SUPERSTARS
of the NFL

Phil Barber

SPORTS ILLUSTRATED is a registered trademark of Time Inc.

Time Inc. Home Entertainment
ISBN: 1-883013-92-5

We welcome your comments and suggestions about SPORTS ILLUSTRATED Books.
Please write to us at:
SPORTS ILLUSTRATED Books
Attention: Book Editors • PO Box 11016 • Des Moines, IA 50336-1016

If you would like to order any of our Hard Cover Collector Edition books, please call us at 1-800-327-6388.
(Monday through Friday, 7:00 a.m.— 8:00 p.m. or Saturday, 7:00 a.m.— 6:00 p.m. Central Time).

NFL Properties Publishing Division
Vice President/Editor-in-Chief: John Wiebusch
General Manager: Bill Barron
Managing Editor: Chuck Garrity, Sr.
Project Editor: Jim Gigliotti

Produced by Lionheart Books, Ltd.
Atlanta, Georgia 30341

Design: Jill Dible

PRINTED IN CANADA

TABLE OF CONTENTS

One Common Denominator and 35 Uncommon Dominators

At first glance, they have no more linking them than 35 random people waiting in line at the Department of Motor Vehicles. Yes, the NFL stars in this book all are outstanding athletes who play the most popular game in America. But they come in more flavors than Jelly Bellies.

They are as compact as running back Emmitt Smith (5 feet 9 inches) and as gargantuan as tackle Tony Boselli (6-7, 322). They are newcomers (wide receiver Randy Moss, 22, and quarterback Peyton Manning, 23, each are in their second season) and established veterans (kicker Morten Andersen, 39, is in his eighteenth NFL season and offensive lineman Bruce Matthews, 38, is in his seventeenth year).

Thirty-five players were selected for this collection, and they have 35 unique stories. Quarterback Troy Aikman grew up in Henryetta, Oklahoma, which is slightly bigger than Kiln, Mississippi, hometown of quarterback Brett Favre. Running back Terrell Davis survived one of San Diego's toughest neighborhoods while Matthews was enjoying suburban life in Arcadia, California. And then there is Andersen, who grew up in Struer, Denmark, his father a psychologist and his mother a teacher.

Quarterback Drew Bledsoe was the Walla Walla Wonder, fingered for stardom in high school and later taken with the first pick of the 1993 draft following his career at Washington State. Tight end Shannon Sharpe attended Savannah State, a Division II school, and was taken in the seventh round in 1990; he caught a grand total of 29 passes his first two NFL seasons. Defensive tackle John Randle wasn't drafted at all. Quarterback Dan Marino was voted to the Pro Bowl as a rookie. It took quarterback Steve Young eight years to get there.

Their personalities are equally diverse. The gregarious Sharpe has yet to find a topic that didn't warrant at least 2,000 words. Contrast him with tight end Ben Coates, who prefers that his actions on the field speak for him.

Cornerback Deion Sanders is known for his $5,000 suits and his hit single, "Must Be the Money." Wide receiver Herman Moore is better known for living in a modest apartment and driving a used pickup truck after signing a lucrative rookie contract.

But if you scratch a little deeper, you are bound to find a common thread that binds these men. When the San Diego Chargers traveled to Rocklin, California, to join the San Francisco 49ers for a dual training camp in 1993, learned observers such as John Madden and Bobby Beathard noted a curious phenomenon: The two guys who consistently expended the most effort were wide receiver Jerry Rice and linebacker Junior Seau—the most talented players also were the hardest workers.

And this is the common denominator you'll find on every page that follows: the drip of sweat. There are a lot of ways to display a Calvinist work ethic. It could be cornerback Aeneas Williams phoning experienced defensive backs to pick their brains about technique and strategy. Maybe it's Randle, dirt-poor child of the East Texas cotton fields, tying a log to his waist and pulling it down the street. Perhaps it's Favre turning out the lights in the empty Green Bay weight room, as he so often does.

All of this might surprise a lot of people. It's easy to dismiss sports stars as gifted freaks of nature who share nothing with the common folk. Then you learn that what really sets these guys apart isn't size or strength or speed (though you can bet they have those qualities in abundance), but raw effort.

Refreshing, isn't it? The same trait that makes a good farmer or a successful engineer also defines an NFL star.

Troy Aikman

Dallas Cowboys

During his five seasons as head coach of the Dallas Cowboys (1989–93), Jimmy Johnson negotiated 46 trades, drafted 54 college players, signed 29 Plan B free agents, and changed offensive coordinators. It was a major overhaul that would take one of sports' most storied franchises to new lows, quickly followed by incredible highs. But one component was never in doubt: quarterback Troy Aikman.

Aikman was the first player ever drafted by Johnson, and he is at the core of the league's most successful team of this decade.

"The best thing that ever happened to Dallas was getting Troy Aikman," says Roger Staubach, whose Cowboys records Aikman has been busy shattering. "They wouldn't have won one Super Bowl in the nineties without him."

For a while, critics wondered if Aikman could win a game. He missed five games with a broken finger in his rookie season and was 0-11 over the remainder of the schedule. He had moments of glory—he passed for 379 yards against Phoenix—but mostly it was a rotten experience for him and the Cowboys. Only the steadiest of players could have bounced back.

Steady? If some quarterbacks play like movie heroes, Aikman plays like the hero's accountant. He can't throw the ball a mile like Drew Bledsoe. He doesn't have John Elway's flair for last-minute heroics. He doesn't break a lot of tackles in the open field.

"I'm not Steve Young, and I'll never be Steve Young," Aikman says. "In our system the ball comes out right away. I don't sit back and hold it."

In Dallas's system, Aikman's directive is simple: Play smart football and keep the boat on course. That is exactly what he has done.

"Troy doesn't make bad decisions," said Norv Turner in 1993, when he was the Cowboys' offensive coordinator. "All the quarterbacks in this league are capable of making big plays. But Troy has reached a point where he doesn't put us in negative situations."

Aikman knows when to throw away the ball or dump off to a back rather than force a deep pass into coverage. His command of the short, timing routes is absolute. "He's very compact and

> "As a receiver, there is not a quarterback in the league you'd rather have throwing to you."
> — Michael Irvin

efficient in his motion," Turner says, "but his biggest strength is accuracy. He's as accurate as any quarterback around, and for a strong-armed guy that's unusual."

Aikman's career completion percentage of 61.81 is the third best in NFL history. His quarterback rating (82.8) ranks eighth on the league's all-time charts. He holds Cowboys records for career attempts (4,011), completions (2,479), yards (28,346), and 3,000-yard seasons (5).

It gets even better in the playoffs. Aikman has been Dallas's Mr. January. In the 1992 postseason, while spurring the Cowboys to victory in Super Bowl XXVII, he completed 61 of 89 passes for 795 yards and 8 touchdowns, with no interceptions. Overall, he has a postseason record of 11-3 as a starter.

"Troy has the whole package," says Michael Irvin, his favorite target. "As a receiver, there is not a quarterback in the league you'd rather have throwing to you."

Aikman was an All-America at UCLA, but his personality is more suited to Henryetta, Oklahoma, the small town where he went to high school. "Troy has a tolerance for bull of somewhere between a second-and-a-half and three seconds," says his agent, Leigh Steinberg.

When it comes to fund raising, the quarterback is much more patient. His Aikman Foundation supports numerous local charities, including the "Aikman End Zone" program, which sets up interactive centers in children's hospitals. His civic efforts brought him the Byron White Humanitarian Award in 1994 and the True Value NFL Man of the Year designation in 1997. The attention is nice, but Aikman remains Aikman.

"The biggest thing about Troy is that he hasn't let superstar status go to his head," Johnson says. "His number-one commitment is to helping the team win. That sets a good example for everybody else."

Yes, Aikman has enjoyed the help of some very

talented teammates. But no one questions who is at the heart of Dallas's offense.

"There are few quarterbacks who can bring their teams to play at a higher level with their own performance," Staubach says. "Troy Aikman is one of them. He'll have a lot of records because he's a great passer. But his main asset is his teammates believe he'll win."

They are justified in their belief. Aikman has started in three Super Bowl victories; no other active quarterback has started in more than one. And that, some would say, is the only statistic that matters at football's most important position.

#8   TROY AIKMAN, Quarterback

YEAR	TEAM	ATT	COMP	PCT	YDS	TD	INT	RATING
1989	Dallas	293	155	52.9	1,749	9	18	55.7
1990	Dallas	399	226	56.6	2,579	11	18	66.6
1991	Dallas	363	237	65.3	2,754	11	10	86.7
1992	Dallas	473	302	63.9	3,445	23	14	89.5
1993	Dallas	392	271	69.1	3,100	15	6	99.0
1994	Dallas	361	233	64.5	2,676	13	12	84.9
1995	Dallas	432	280	64.8	3,304	16	7	93.6
1996	Dallas	465	296	63.7	3,126	12	13	80.1
1997	Dallas	518	292	56.4	3,283	19	12	78.0
1998	Dallas	315	187	59.4	2,330	12	5	88.5
CAREER TOTALS		4,011	2,479	61.8	28,346	141	115	82.8

Morten Andersen

In 1995, the New Orleans Saints learned that hell hath no fury like a kicker scorned. Hoping to squeeze under the salary cap by forcing him to accept a smaller number, they cut Morten Andersen two days before the start of training camp. But Andersen had no interest in being down-salaried. He contacted the Saints' arch rival, the Atlanta Falcons, and was in a new uniform within 24 hours.

New Orleans fans were shocked. They weren't just losing the leading scorer in club history. They were losing one of their most popular citizens. Andersen had raised more than $400,000 for Children's Hospital through his Kicks for Kids program, and his good looks made him something of a heart throb. A poster of Andersen in a cutoff jersey and shorts sold 16,000 copies, and *New Orleans Magazine* named him one of the city's 10 most eligible bachelors.

Of course, some people were thrilled with the move—namely, the Falcons veterans who had watched Andersen beat their team five times with last-minute kicks. "You can't imagine how depressing it was to watch that guy destroy us game after game," linebacker Jessie Tuggle says.

The Saints soon would know the feeling. In the first of the rivals' two games of 1995, Andersen made 4 of 4 field-goal attempts, the last from 21 yards with 4:02 remaining in overtime to give Atlanta a 27-24 victory. "That was a sweet kick," Andersen said of the game winner. "It really gave me a sense of closure. It helped me exorcise a lot of demons."

The demons were ducking for cover when the teams met again in December. Andersen again was 4 for 4, and this time 3 of them were from beyond 50 yards (55, 55, and 51). It was the first time in NFL history someone had kicked three 50-yard field goals in one game.

As if the Saints had forgotten, Andersen has tremendous leg strength. He is, in fact, an exemplary athlete who was a gymnast and a long jumper in high school in Struer, Denmark, and who narrowly missed making the Danish junior national soccer team.

Andersen never saw an American football until he came to the United States as a 17-year-old exchange student. He was hanging around practice at Ben Davis High School in Indianapolis when the coach spotted him nailing 50-yard kicks, and that was the start of a dream career.

Since joining the Saints as a fourth-round draft choice in 1983, Andersen has established NFL records for scoring in consecutive games (238 and counting), 50-yard field goals in a career (35), 50-

yard kicks in a season (5, in 1995), 100-point seasons (12), and Pro Bowl appearances by a kicker (7). He has two of the five longest field goals in NFL history, and his kickoffs routinely sail past the goal line.

But it is his 25 game-winning kicks that are most impressive.

"Morten has a different button from most kickers," says June Jones, former head coach of the Falcons. "More often than not, when the game is on the line, most kickers are pacing, really nervous. Morten is the first kicker I've had who *wants* to kick with the game on the line. What Joe Montana is to quarterbacks, Morten is to kickers."

For Andersen, it isn't so much containing his anxiety as refusing to acknowledge it in the first place. "Doubt will make you unemployed very quickly," he says. "That's why I'm so meticulous about my preparation."

Andersen is a big proponent of visualization. He walks himself through various kicking scenarios at every prac-

> "Morten is the first kicker I've had who *wants* to kick with the game on the line. What Joe Montana is to quarterbacks, Morten is to kickers."
> — June Jones

tice. All of them end the same way, with the ball traveling end-over-end through the uprights. He is, by all accounts, a cerebral man. He speaks four languages. He was an academic All-America at Michigan State, with a double major in communications and German and a double minor in marketing and French.

Perhaps it is his educational background and rich well of life experiences (he hiked the Himalayas with his father Erik a few years ago) that allow Andersen to put his trade in healthy perspective. "There are one billion Chinese people who couldn't care less about what I do," he likes to say. "My little egocentric endeavors are insignificant. They certainly don't change world events."

Or as his mother Hanne once put it: "It's not really all that important what he does. He kicks a football."

At least Mrs. Andersen can rest assured that her son kicks that ball as well as anyone ever has.

#5 MORTEN ANDERSEN, Kicker

YEAR	TEAM	XPM	XPA	FGM	FGA	LONG	PTS
1982	New Orleans	6	6	2	5	45	12
1983	New Orleans	37	38	18	24	52	91
1984	New Orleans	34	34	20	27	53	94
1985	New Orleans	27	29	31	35	55	120
1986	New Orleans	30	30	26	30	53	108
1987	New Orleans	37	37	28	36	52	121
1988	New Orleans	32	33	26	36	51	110
1989	New Orleans	44	45	20	29	49	104
1990	New Orleans	29	29	21	27	52	92
1991	New Orleans	38	38	25	32	60	113
1992	New Orleans	33	34	29	34	52	120
1993	New Orleans	33	33	28	35	56	117
1994	New Orleans	32	32	28	39	48	116
1995	Atlanta	29	30	31	37	59	122
1996	Atlanta	31	31	22	29	54	97
1997	Atlanta	35	35	23	27	55	104
1998	Atlanta	51	52	23	28	53	120
CAREER TOTALS		558	566	401	510	60	1,761

Jamal Anderson

Atlanta Falcons

Jamal Anderson wasn't exactly awed by the NFL stars who greeted him upon his arrival in the league. After all, brushes with celebrity had been part of his life for as long as he could remember.

How many other children had boxing legend Muhammad Ali waiting in the delivery room when they were born, or immortal running back Jim Brown pacing the sidelines during their Pop Warner football games? How many kids stepped around Arsenio Hall as he lay sleeping on the living room floor, or got a haircut from NBA guard Byron Scott, or heard bedtime stories read by Donna Summer?

"Being raised around celebrities inspired Jamal to shoot for something big, to strive to be the best at whatever path in life he chose," says his father, James Anderson, who got to know the big shots through his work as a high-priced bodyguard. "And to make sure that if and when he got to the top, he handled it with class."

Of course, Jamal's parents wouldn't have it any other way. "I remind him that he's the Flavor of the Week," says his mother, Zenobia. "There's never been any celebrity in my house, and we're not going to start now."

Jamal became the Flavor of the Week sometime during the 1998 season, when he carried the Atlanta Falcons to an unexpected appearance in Super Bowl XXXIII. Anderson was both the physical and emotional cornerstone of that team. He rushed for a gaudy 1,846 yards on 410 carries (the most in NFL history), and he even invented a dance—the Dirty Bird—that became to the 1998 Falcons what the Super Bowl Shuffle was to the 1985 Bears.

It was one of the strangest ascents the NFL had seen in some time.

After playing at Moorpark (California) Junior College and the University of Utah, Anderson lasted into the seventh round of the 1994 NFL draft. When he got to training camp and spied his name at the bottom of the depth chart on a blackboard, he circled it and drew an arrow to the top. But such confidence seemed unfounded by the end of his rookie season, when he had been outgained by all those celebrities with whom he had mingled as a child. Anderson's final numbers: 2 carries for minus-1 yard.

In retrospect, it's clear that all Anderson needed was a chance. Opportunity came in 1996, when Atlanta moved one of his mentors, Craig (Ironhead)

> "He's a hard guy to tackle because he doesn't give you much of a target to hit. All you see is helmet, shoulder pads, and knees, and those things are no fun to hit."

Heyward to fullback, and installed Anderson as the starter at tailback. It wasn't long before players and fans around the league took notice of the powerful back with the gap-toothed smile.

Anderson had the first of three consecutive 1,000-yard seasons in 1996, gaining 1,055 yards. After rushing for 1,002 yards in 1997, he set a franchise record for rushing yards in 1998 while also leading all NFC players with 14 rushing touchdowns. He was named to the Pro Bowl for the first time.

Anderson runs with a style unlike any other ball carrier. His massive thighs (he can squat 670 pounds) and quick acceleration draw comparisons to the great Earl Campbell. At the same time, his balletic spin moves and herky-jerky motion sometimes look more like Barry Sanders.

"He has tremendous power," Falcons head coach Dan Reeves says. "He's a hard guy to tackle because he doesn't give you much of a target to hit. All you see is helmet, shoulder pads, and knees, and those things are no fun to hit."

"Just give me the ball and get out of the way," Anderson says.

George Teague, the Cowboys' veteran safety, was late in accepting Anderson's suggestion. They met head to head at Dallas's 6-yard line during a 1996 contest, and Teague wound up offering a reasonable impersonation of a corn tortilla. "What's the old saying, 'Hey, somebody get the license number of that truck?'" the defender said after the game. "Well, this was more like being run over by the whole convoy."

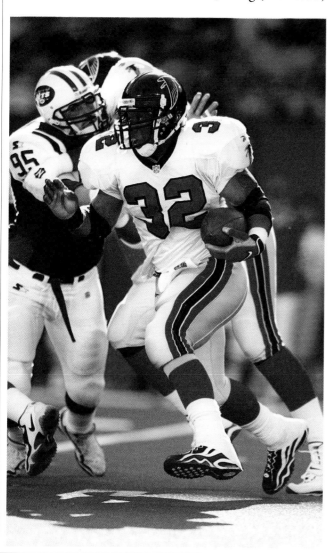

#32 JAMAL ANDERSON, Running Back

YEAR	TEAM	RUSHING				RECEIVING			
		NO.	YDS.	AVG.	TD	NO.	YDS.	AVG.	TD
1994	Atlanta	2	-1	-0.5	0	0	0	—	0
1995	Atlanta	39	161	4.1	1	4	42	10.5	0
1996	Atlanta	232	1,055	4.5	5	49	473	9.7	1
1997	Atlanta	290	1,002	3.5	7	29	284	9.8	3
1998	Atlanta	410	1,846	4.5	14	27	319	11.8	2
CAREER TOTALS		973	4,063	4.2	27	109	1,118	10.3	6

Jerome Bettis

Pittsburgh Steelers

Dermontti Dawson, the Steelers' Pro Bowl center, remembers a goal-line play at Cincinnati in 1997. It was fourth down from the 1 with Pittsburgh trailing 7-6, and the handoff went to Jerome Bettis. "I just looked up and saw him for a second, and his legs were going a hundred miles per hour," Dawson says. "I knew nothing was going to stop him from getting into the end zone."

Bettis got his six points and the Steelers went on to win 26-10. It wasn't exactly the NFL play of the year, but it was the perfect illustration of the Jerome Bettis style of football. His nickname is "The Bus"—it has been since he played at Notre Dame—and if you value your health you are encouraged to stay out from under his wheels.

"You'd better stop Bettis before he gets started," says Ozzie Newsome, Baltimore's vice president of player personnel. "Once he gets through the line and squares up, he causes some problems. There aren't too many people in the secondary who want to spend their Sunday afternoons tackling Jerome Bettis."

He is 5 feet 11 inches, 250 pounds, with the thighs of a Kodiak bear and the gut of a piano mover. Bettis has surprisingly nimble moves, too, but the basis of his game is the straight-ahead rumble.

"After you tackle him you're laughing and joking with him," veteran NFL safety Eugene Robinson says.

"But on your way to the huddle you're thinking, 'Oh, boy, I'm in trouble.'"

Bettis was an NFL star from the outset. He rushed for 1,429 yards as a rookie in 1993 and 1,025 yards in his second season, both with the Rams. But he fell out of favor with the Rams and his carries declined.

The usually jovial runner was at an emotional low, but he was recharged by a trade to Pittsburgh in 1996. Steelers director of football operations Tom Donahoe heard nothing but praise about Bettis. "He's a real friendly kid," says Joe Moore, the former Notre Dame assistant who recruited Bettis. "He's easygoing off the field, easy to get along with, and has a nice personality."

So for the price of second- and fourth-round picks, the Steelers got a workhorse ball carrier. And Bettis, only 24 at the time, got a new lease on life.

"We had to have him," Pittsburgh head coach

"After you tackle him you're laughing and joking with him," veteran NFL safety Eugene Robinson says. "But on your way to the huddle you're thinking, 'Oh, boy, I'm in trouble.'"

Bill Cowher says. "You win championships with people, and they don't come any finer than Jerome."

Bettis has flourished in the Steelers' game plan. He was second to Denver's Terrell Davis among AFC rushers with 1,431 yards in 1996 and 1,665 in 1997. The latter figure was a mere 25 yards shy of Barry Foster's club record, and Bettis sat out one game. He had his fifth 1,000-yard season in 1998 with 1,185. He also has 23 touchdowns in three seasons.

"His style is made to order for what they want to do," Indianapolis defensive tackle Tony McCoy says. "He is going to pound on you. He makes them a tough team to beat."

For his part, Bettis extends the comfort zone from the offense to the entire city. "I'm a blue-collar player, and this is a blue-collar town," he says.

How blue-collar is Bettis? His second-favorite game is bowling. When he was a kid, his mother Gladys took him to Detroit's Central City Lanes, mainly to keep him off the streets. Bettis grew to love the alleys. He averages about 200, and in 1995 he rolled a perfect 300 during a pro-am event in Michigan.

Meanwhile, Steelers' fans have gleefully adopted Bettis. They buy Bus caps and T-shirts like they once snapped up Terrible Towels. When St. Louis came to town in 1996, someone hung a banner at Three Rivers Stadium that read: "Blitzburg Thanks the Rams for the Gift That Keeps on Giving 100 Yards a Game: No. 36."

Bettis responded with 129 yards in a 42-6 victory.

To show appreciation for his full-throttle career, Bettis has lavished gifts upon his offensive linemen and Tim Lester, the fullback who blocked for him with both the Rams and the Steelers. He has bought them big-screen televisions, expensive dinners, and trips to Honolulu for the Pro Bowl. At least one of those linemen, however, doesn't see what all the fuss is about.

"As hard as he runs," former guard Will Wolford says, "he's his own blocker."

#36 JEROME BETTIS, Running Back

YEAR	TEAM	RUSHING				RECEIVING			
		NO	YDS	AVG	TD	NO	YDS	AVG	TD
1993	L.A. Rams	294	1,429	4.9	7	26	244	9.4	0
1994	L.A. Rams	319	1,025	3.2	3	31	293	9.5	1
1995	St. Louis	183	637	3.5	3	18	106	5.9	0
1996	Pittsburgh	320	1,431	4.5	11	22	122	5.5	0
1997	Pittsburgh	375	1,665	4.4	7	15	110	7.3	2
1998	Pittsburgh	316	1,185	3.8	3	16	90	5.6	0
CAREER TOTALS		1,807	7,372	4.1	34	128	965	7.5	3

Drew Bledsoe

New England Patriots

If you had to pinpoint the date when Patriots quarterback Drew Bledsoe "arrived," it would be November 13, 1994. On that day the Patriots, already staggering at 3-6, fell behind Minnesota 20-0. Coach Bill Parcells had seen enough. With less than a minute left in the first half, he ordered a hurry-up offense — and Bledsoe went wild. In the latter stages of the game he passed on 34 consecutive plays. He completed his first 6 passes in overtime and hit Kevin Turner for the winning touchdown at 4:10 of the extra period.

Bledsoe finished the game with NFL records for attempts (70) and completions (45). By the end of 1994, he had set a league mark with 691 attempts in a season. He has been one of the sport's most productive quarterbacks ever since.

Anything less, of course, would be considered a failure for Bledsoe, who was fitted for a superstar's cleats years ago. His football background started early: at age 3 he attended a football camp led by his father, Mac (who would later become his high school coach). In the seventh grade, Drew was beaten out for the starting quarterback position; it never would happen again.

By the time Bledsoe got to Washington State he was the Walla Walla Wonder, a strapping phenom

who was destined for the NFL. And when he became the first pick in the 1993 draft, he brought a ton of expectations with him.

Bob Ryan, a *Boston Globe* columnist, welcomed

Bledsoe by writing, "Only injury will prevent Drew Bledsoe from becoming the Patriots' answer to Teddy, Bobby, and Larry."

Ryan was referring to the Boston Holy Trinity of baseball's Ted Williams, hockey's Bobby Orr, and basketball's Larry Bird. When Bledsoe heard the prediction, he rolled his eyes and said, "I wish people would wait until I do something before making these comparisons."

He's done a few things since then, such as taking his team to the playoffs four times in six seasons, when it hadn't been to postseason play in the six years prior to his arrival. Twice he has thrown for more than 4,000 yards (in 1994 and

1996). After the '94 season he became the youngest quarterback ever to play in the Pro Bowl. (Dan Marino was 7 months younger when he was voted to his first Pro Bowl, but a knee injury kept him out of the game.) During a seven-game span in 1995, Bledsoe set a club record by throwing 179 consecutive passes without an interception.

"He can throw any kind of pass," former Patriots quarterback Steve Grogan says. "Drew reminds me of a young Marino. He has a knack of seeing the field

> "He can throw any kind of pass. Drew reminds me of a young Marino. He has a knack of seeing the field and delivering the ball."
> — Steve Grogan

and delivering the ball. He also seems to have a real good head on his shoulders. He hasn't let his successes affect him or his failures drag him down."

Physically dragging him down is a difficult problem. He is 6 feet 5 inches and 233 pounds, and was rugged enough to start 58 consecutive games between 1995-98. But Bledsoe has persistent detractors. They say that he forces the ball into coverage and that he throws too many interceptions. More significantly, they claim he tends to self-destruct in critical games. The facts say otherwise.

Bledsoe and the Patriots lost to Green Bay in Super Bowl XXXI, but could anyone have beaten the Packers that day? Anyway, at 24 he was the third-youngest quarterback to start in a Super Bowl. What's more, Bledsoe has a career record of 15-7 in December, the NFL's make-or-break month. He's superb in the two-minute drill, and last season rallied the Patriots from behind by throwing the winning touchdown pass in the final 30 seconds of back-to-back games. That's performance under pressure.

"He's one of the few people I know on earth who has an inner calm," says Bledsoe's agent, Leigh Steinberg.

That serene posture helps Bledsoe, the prototype quarterback of the nineties, keep his life and work in perspective.

"Win or lose," Bledsoe says, "when I come home my dogs will jump all over me."

#11 DREW BLEDSOE, Quarterback

YEAR	TEAM	ATT	COMP	PCT	YDS	TD	INT	RATING
1993	New England	429	214	49.9	2,494	15	15	65.0
1994	New England	691	400	57.9	4,555	25	27	73.6
1995	New England	636	323	50.8	3,507	13	16	63.7
1996	New England	623	373	59.9	4,086	27	15	83.7
1997	New England	522	314	60.2	3,706	28	15	87.7
1998	New England	481	263	54.7	3,633	20	14	80.9
CAREER TOTALS		3,382	1,887	55.8	21,981	128	102	75.7

Tony Boselli

Angi Aylor had been dating Tony Boselli for about four months, and she knew he was a football player. She just didn't know if he was any good. He told her he was a "fringe player." Then Aylor went to a Fourth of July party and met a couple of players from Stanford. "My boyfriend plays for USC," she told them, "but you probably haven't heard of him. His name is Tony Boselli."

The Cardinal players' jaws dropped. They directed Aylor to the nearest newsstand, where she picked up a copy of a college football preview magazine. Her boyfriend was on the cover. Inside, the magazine said he might be the best player in the conference.

Aylor later became Miss California 1994, and after that Mrs. Tony Boselli. And she still can't believe the way she was duped. Only an offensive tackle could have pulled it off.

But Boselli is so good, so unique, that even the trenches no longer can hide him. At 27, he might be the best offensive lineman in the NFL.

"He is the guy who I've seen come out recently who will be around a long, long time," legendary tackle Anthony Muñoz says. "It's all technique. You can be big, strong, and athletic, but if you have poor technique you can't block anybody. Tony has it. I've watched him. He's great already, and he'll only get better."

Muñoz, of course, preceded Boselli at USC. So did offensive linemen such as Bruce Matthews, Roy Foster, and Don Mosebar. And yet John Robinson, who coached all of them, described Boselli as "the best college lineman I've ever had."

At 6 feet 7 inches, 324 pounds, his appeal was obvious to NFL scouts. But when Jaguars head coach Tom Coughlin met with Boselli and watched him work out, it wasn't the massive frame

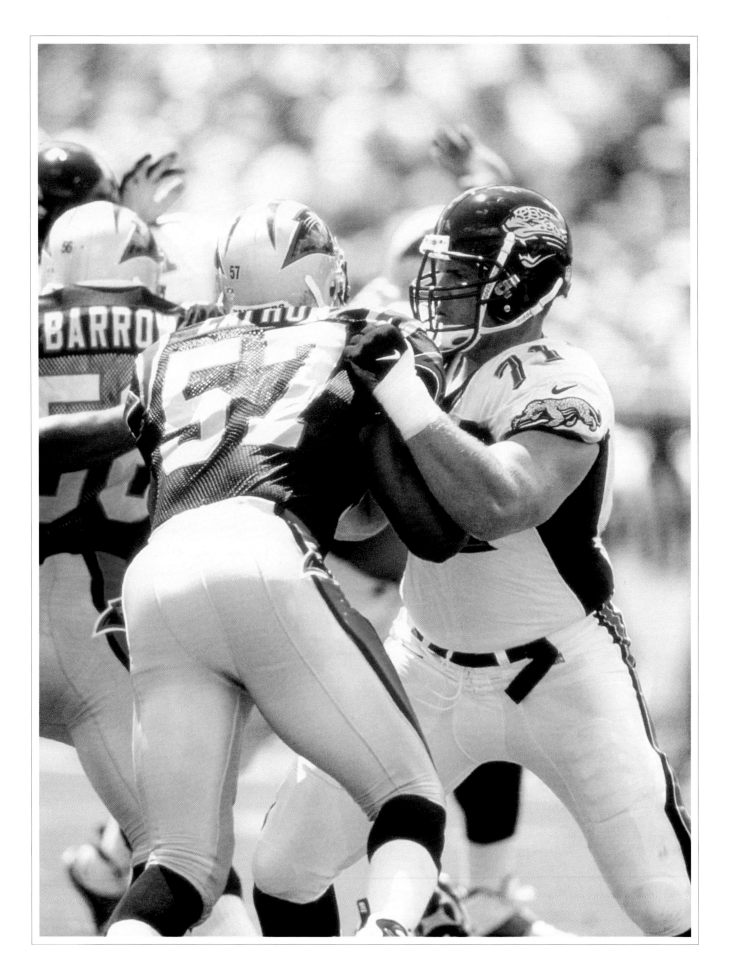

that left him shaking his head. "The key for me was the maturity he had that was beyond his years — the poise, the attitude," the coach says. "Tony brought a lot to the table."

So Coughlin and the Jaguars took Boselli with the second pick in 1995, making him the highest-drafted offensive lineman since Tony Mandarich in 1989. More significantly, Boselli became the inaugural draft choice in the history of the Jacksonville franchise. "He's the cornerstone," Coughlin said as the team signed him to the richest contract ever for a rookie offensive lineman: $17 million over seven years.

It was money well spent. At left tackle, Boselli routinely faces the NFL's most devastating pass rushers—and he routinely leaves them frustrated and fruitless. This never was more evident than in the 1996 playoffs, when the Jaguars took to the road to play the Bills and Broncos. In those two games Boselli went up against Bruce Smith and Alfred Williams, who had combined for 26½ sacks in the regular season. (Smith was consensus NFL defensive player of the year.) Neither of them laid a hand on Mark Brunell, and Jacksonville emerged with consecutive upset victories.

"Tony is a very, very large human being," Coughlin says, "but he moves with the grace of someone smaller. Here's a man fifty pounds heavier than any premier NFL pass rusher, but he has the athleticism, maneuverability, and speed to compete with them."

Boselli always has been known as a technically superb pass blocker. It was his run blocking that some questioned, and so that is where he worked—and worked, and worked. He practiced his leverage and his footwork. He lowered his stance and rehearsed his steps until he was a force on the run, too.

Where did Boselli get such a work ethic? Maybe it was the two summers he spent gardening, baling hay, and rounding up calves for the Benedictine nuns of the Abbey of St. Walburga, just outside Boulder, Colorado. "There were days at the con-

> **"Tony is a very, very large human being," Coughlin says, "but he moves with the grace of someone smaller."**

vent when the nuns worked me harder than the USC coaching staff did," Boselli says.

More likely, it has to do with his churning desire to be the best. "He's a Pro Bowl player," Jacksonville guard Ben Coleman says, "but you still see him after practice, working on different techniques, studying the opponent because he wants to be able to take care of his business."

Boselli knows there is little that separates the good NFL players from the great ones these days. "The position I play is all about consistency," says the man who recently went more than 36 games without missing an offensive play. "The only thing people remember is your last game and your last year.

"That's all I concern myself with: How am I going to play in the next game?"

Tim Brown

Jeff Hostetler was a hard-nosed overachiever who excelled at throwing on the run. Jeff George is a classic dropback passer with a strong arm and a mercurial temperament. The two quarterbacks couldn't have more disparate styles, but they have one thing in common (beyond their first name): They both name Tim Brown as the best receiver with whom they've played.

"He has size, speed, the ability to run with the ball, and a sense of where to find open holes," Hostetler says as evidence.

"He can do it all," George says. "He can play outside, he can play slot. You can put him in the backfield and run routes that way. He's got what it takes."

Brown has played catch with a lot of quarterbacks during his tenure in Oakland—Jay Schroeder, Todd Marinovich, Vince Evans are a few more examples—and all of them would likely rank him at the top. They simply don't come much better equipped than number 81.

Some players are game-breakers, others are reliable possession receivers. Brown is one of the few who can fill both roles. He is a dangerous runner after the catch, too. And this is after a 1989 knee injury that, he claims, permanently impaired his speed.

Before that setback, everything

had come easy for the kid who once dreamed of being "Twinkletoes Brown," star Cowboys running back. He was an All-America runner for Woodrow Wilson High School in Dallas, and he spent four storied years at Notre Dame. He won the 1987

Heisman Trophy and departed with school records for receiving yards (2,493), kickoff-return yards (1,613), and all-purpose yards (5,024).

The Raiders made Brown the first wide receiver taken in a rich 1988 draft that included the likes of Sterling Sharpe, Michael Irvin, and Anthony Miller, and he made the NFL seem like nothing more than a giant playground. Brown finished the year as the NFL leader in kick-off returns (a 26.8-yard average), the AFC leader in punt-return yardage (444), and the Raiders' leader in receptions (43). His 2,317 all-purpose yards broke the

"He'll freeze a guy like he's in slow motion," former Raiders linebacker Rob Fredrickson says. "Then he has a sudden burst of speed. He's great at changing speeds and changing directions."

league rookie record formerly held by Gale Sayers.

But in the first game of 1989 Brown tore his posterior cruciate and medial collateral ligaments. He missed the rest of the season and didn't start the next two as he regained his strength.

Now that seems like ancient history. Brown has led the AFC in receiving yardage in four of the last six seasons. He had his best year ever in 1997, when George found him 104 times for 1,408 yards. Both figures were club records, and the reception total tied him (with Herman Moore) for the NFL lead.

Some defenses will even send a linebacker out wide to hamper Brown at the line. The Raiders counter by frequently sending him in motion, but often it is Brown's resourcefulness that gets him free. His signature "double move"—fake inside, fake back outside, cut upfield—has been known to leave defensive backs twisted into abstract art pieces.

"He'll freeze a guy like he's in slow motion," former Raiders linebacker Rob Fredrickson says. "Then he has a sudden burst of speed. He's great at changing speeds and changing directions."

At least opposing special teams don't have to worry about him anymore. Brown was a two-time Pro Bowl choice as a kick returner, but he relinquished kickoff returns long ago, and he handed over his punt-return chores in 1997. Before passing the torch, however, Brown returned more punts (301) than any other man in NFL history. He still is the only Raiders player ever to score on a reception, a handoff, a punt return, and a kickoff return.

Yes, Twinkletoes Brown has won just about every honor imaginable for a football player. But the big one has eluded him. He never has won a championship, not at any level. It is a pursuit that consumes him, and if he has to carry the Raiders there on his back, that's fine with him.

"I like being the go-to guy," Brown says. "It puts pressure on me, but that's why you play this game."

You would expect opponents to double-team Brown—and they do. That constantly opens up routes for tight end Rickey Dudley and fellow wide receiver James Jett, but it doesn't necessarily ensure that Brown will be shut down.

"He's one of the only receivers I know who can get open against double coverage," Jets cornerback Aaron Glenn says. "He can make moves and get open. I don't know how he does it, but he does."

#81 TIM BROWN, Wide Receiver

YEAR	TEAM	NO	YDS	AVG	TD
1988	L.A. Raiders	43	725	16.9	5
1989	L.A. Raiders	1	8	8.0	0
1990	L.A. Raiders	18	265	14.7	3
1991	L.A. Raiders	36	554	15.4	5
1992	L.A. Raiders	49	693	14.1	7
1993	L.A. Raiders	80	1,180	14.8	7
1994	L.A. Raiders	89	1,309	14.7	9
1995	Oakland	89	1,342	15.1	10
1996	Oakland	90	1,104	12.3	9
1997	Oakland	104	1,408	13.5	5
1998	Oakland	81	1,012	12.5	9
CAREER TOTALS		680	9,600	14.1	69

Mark Brunell

Jacksonville Jaguars

During the 1996 season, a television analyst asked Jacksonville quarterback Mark Brunell how it felt to have one of the NFL's best left tackles, Tony Boselli, protecting his blindside. One problem: Brunell is a left-handed passer. Boselli protects his frontside.

The analyst can be forgiven for his oversight, for at that point Brunell still was relatively unknown, even as he authored a season that would make him the first man since Johnny Unitas in 1962 to lead all NFL quarterbacks in both passing yards (4,367) and rushing yards (396). The anonymity wouldn't last much longer, however.

In the first round of the AFC playoffs, Brunell led the Jaguars to victory over the Bills in Rich Stadium, where no visiting team ever had won a postseason game. In the second round, he sparked a 30-27 upset of the mighty Broncos, an outcome some called pro football's biggest postseason upset since Super Bowl III.

"We never faced a quarterback like that before," Denver defensive end Alfred Williams said after the game.

They also never wanted to see another. Brunell repeatedly squirmed away from pass rushers that day. He zipped downfield for big first downs and launched dead-on passes into the end zone, showing a national televi-

sion audience what the Jaguars fans had been seeing for more than a year. A month later he increased the exposure by earning most-valuable-player honors in the Pro Bowl.

Brunell had been such a secret because, before

coming to Jacksonville in April, 1995, circumstances had conspired to keep him in the background. He led the Washington Huskies to a Rose Bowl victory as a college sophomore, but he injured his knee during the following spring practice and wound up splitting time with Billy Joe Hobert.

When the Green Bay Packers drafted Brunell in the third round in 1993, he found himself playing second fiddle to the maestro, Brett Favre. Brunell

never started in two seasons. He passed for only 95 yards.

But some NFL people never let him fall off the radar screen. One of them was Jaguars head coach Tom Coughlin, who was busy building a franchise from scratch. "I had spent much of the past year trying to find a quarterback who would be a leader in all ways," Coughlin says. "Without question, of the players who might be available, he was the guy

I wanted as the quarterback of the future here."

The Jaguars got Brunell for the paltry price of a third- and a fifth-round draft choice. It was the first trade ever made by Jacksonville, and it may go down as its best. In the fifth week of the Jaguars' first season, Brunell led the franchise to its first victory—17-16 over the Oilers—and a year later he carried it to the AFC Championship Game.

Brunell has been compared to Steve Young, except he isn't wasting much of his youth waiting for a Joe Montana to retire. Brunell is a fearless leader, a good touch passer, and a sensational scrambler who has been clocked at 4.58 seconds in the 40-

yard dash. "When he is running free, it frightens you to death," Chiefs cornerback Cris Dishman says.

"Sometimes I have to stop to watch him," Jacksonville wide receiver Jimmy Smith says.

Off the field, however, the loose cannon becomes a strict adherent of Christian canons. Brunell leads 15 to 20 Jaguars teammates in regular Bible study. He had a 3.92 grade-point average in high school. He is a devoted family man who worked construction and roofing jobs as a college senior to support his wife and child.

Brunell needed all of his inner strength in 1997. He suffered a severe knee injury in August, and after he returned (ahead of schedule, thanks to four hours a day of rehabilitative work) he suffered a severely bruised buttock and a dislocated middle finger on his passing hand. When he played, the tender knee took away much of the mobility that had made him so dangerous.

Instead of despairing, Brunell focused on becoming a better dropback passer. He finished the season first in the AFC with a passer rating of 91.2, throwing 18 touchdown passes against 7 interceptions.

"He has his faith and his family and football, and that is all he needs," Jaguars senior vice president Michael Huyghue says. "Some people need training wheels on their bike before thay can ride. Mark just got right on his bike and started doing tricks."

#8 MARK BRUNELL, Quarterback

YEAR	TEAM	ATT	COMP	PCT	YDS	TD	INT	RATING
1993	Green Bay — Did not play							
1994	Green Bay	27	12	44.4	95	0	0	53.8
1995	Jacksonville	346	201	58.1	2,168	15	7	82.6
1996	Jacksonville	557	353	63.4	4,367	19	20	84.0
1997	Jacksonville	435	264	60.7	3,281	18	7	91.2
1998	Jacksonville	354	208	58.8	2,601	20	9	89.9
CAREER TOTALS		1,719	1,038	60.4	12,512	72	43	86.3

Cris Carter

It wasn't as cheap as the phone call that supposedly brought Hall of Fame quarterback Johnny Unitas to Baltimore in 1956, but the $100 the Vikings spent to acquire Cris Carter in 1990 has to be rated one of the great sports deals of the century.

Carter, who had played three seasons in Philadelphia, suddenly found himself on the waiver wire the week before the start of the 1990 season.

Stunned by being waived, Carter rededicated himself to the game. Known for less-than-heroic efforts on the practice field, he vowed to work harder. He stopped eating red meat. He gave up alcohol. He cut down on sweets and began a determined fitness regimen.

Carter displayed the same dedication off the field. By 1995, he was accepting the Bart Starr Award from Athletes in Action for outstanding leadership and character on and off the field. He was ordained a minister in 1996. He has committed much of his time to local charities (largely through the Carter-White Charitable Foundation, which he founded with safety William White), and he has become the Vikings' unquestioned locker-room leader.

"I thank him for my success," says teammate Jake Reed, another productive receiver. "He makes me sit down and think about my life. One thing about Cris: He's not going to tell you what you *want* to hear; he'll tell you what you *need* to hear."

Happily, Carter's career has blossomed along with his improved attitude. At the beginning of the 1994 season he was considered a good receiver. By the end of the year he was hailed as one of the game's big-time performers. Carter set an NFL record (since broken) with 122 catches in 1994, and has followed it with totals of 122 (again), 96, 89, and 78. He owns Vikings records for career

receptions (745), yards (8,997), and touchdown catches (82).

"Cris is like the small forward in basketball," Vikings head coach Dennis Green says. "He always wants the ball: 'Get it to me down low. Get it to me coming off the post. Get it to me in the lane. Get it to me on an Alley-Oop. Just get it to me because if you get it to me I'll

make the play.' That's his approach to the game."

The basketball analogy is an appropriate one, since Carter's oldest brother Butch starred under Bobby Knight at Indiana and played seven seasons in the NBA.

Cris showed some court moves himself when he won the 1995 Foot Locker Slam Dunk Competition. It

is that leaping ability, along with his size (6 feet 3 inches, 208 pounds), that make Carter the most dangerous goal-line receiver in the game. He led the NFL in touchdown receptions two of the last four seasons, with 17 in 1995 and 13 in 1997 (he also had three 2-point conversions in 1997).

"You never want to cover him inside your twenty-yard line because he has such great leaping ability," Raiders cornerback Eric Allen says. "The only thing you can do is play the ball and hope you can get it before he does."

And even when the opponent appears to have position, Carter often finds a way to make the catch. "Cris is very acrobatic," says Jerry Rhome, his former receivers coach. "It doesn't seem to bother him to have defenders around. He can jump through the roof, and he has stretching ability. He can make his arms long and his hands long."

Expandable digits? Hey, anything seems possible

for a man who has risen from the NFL scrap heap, stretching his life and career to their full potential.

#80 CRIS CARTER, Wide Receiver

YEAR	TEAM	NO	YDS	AVG	TD
1987	Philadelphia	5	84	16.8	2
1988	Philadelphia	39	761	19.5	6
1989	Philadelphia	45	605	13.4	11
1990	Minnesota	27	413	15.3	3
1991	Minnesota	72	962	13.4	5
1992	Minnesota	53	681	12.9	6
1993	Minnesota	86	1,071	12.5	9
1994	Minnesota	122	1,256	10.3	7
1995	Minnesota	122	1,371	11.2	17
1996	Minnesota	96	1,163	12.1	10
1997	Minnesota	89	1,069	12.0	13
1998	Minnesota	78	1,011	13.0	12
CAREER TOTALS		834	10,447	12.5	101

Ben Coates

New England Patriots

In 1991, the Patriots' brain trust got word of a tight end prospect in Salisbury, North Carolina. The player was big, fast, and generally athletic, the scouts reported. But he still was considered a gamble because of his lack of experience. He hadn't played football until his senior year of high school. He put aside his pads during his junior year of college to concentrate on basketball and track. And he faced practically no credible competition at Division II Livingstone College.

"Dante [Scarnecchia] was coaching tight ends at the time, and we sent him down there," says Joe Mendes, New England's personnel director in '91. "We told him, 'You don't have to work him out. You don't have to watch any film. Just spend a day with him and find out, can you coach him?'

"So Dante works him out, and then he's even more in love with him. He comes back and says, 'No question, this guy can play for me.'"

As it turns out, the young tight end—Ben Coates—could play for anybody in the universe.

"He's a nightmare to cover," says Todd Collins, a former Patriots linebacker who had to take on Coates at practice. "He's so big that he can push you off him, and he can catch everything high. [Coates is 6 feet 5 inches, 245 pounds.] You can try to use two people, three people on him, but Drew [Bledsoe] throws to him anyway because Ben is like a vacuum cleaner when the ball comes his way. No matter who's doing what, he sucks it in."

Former New England cornerback Jimmy

Hitchcock is more succinct in his assessment: "He's the best player I've ever seen."

Coates, a fifth-round draft choice in 1991, had little impact during his first two years in the league. But his development was helped by the arrival of two men, Bill Parcells and Drew Bledsoe, in 1993. Parcells, the new head coach, had a history of relying on big tight ends. Bledsoe, then a rookie quarterback, opened up the field with his cannon-strong arm. Parcells gave Coates a chance; Bledsoe helped make him a star.

Coates led the Patriots with 53 receptions in '93, but it was the next season that sent him into a higher orbit. He was sensational in 1994, catching 96 passes (most ever for a tight end), good for 1,174 yards and 7 touchdowns. Suddenly, the secret was out.

"I don't know where that guy came from," Bills

running back Thurman Thomas said after a game that year, "but you can send him to Hawaii right now."

Actually, Coates had to wait until February to play in the Pro Bowl, but he's been back every year since. He leads all NFL tight ends with 375 catches and 36 touchdowns over the last five seasons, and he currently ranks second on the Patriots' career receptions list with 458. He already holds club records for most catches in a season (96), most in a game (12, at Indianapolis in 1994), and most consecutive games with a reception (63).

"Any quarterback in the league would love to throw to the guy," Bledsoe says. "He's always going to catch the ball, and then one out of every two

> "He's a tight end who's like an extra offensive lineman, and a tight end who's like an extra wide receiver," Bledsoe says.

passes he's going to break two or three tackles and make a big play."

Coates is not one of these wide-receivers-by-another-name who flourish in the West Coast offense. He also can be a devastating blocker—which makes it all the more shocking the first time you get a good look at his speed.

"Like in practice," Hitchcock once said "I'm watching him get by me, and then the ball is thrown and I'm thinking, 'There's no way he's going to get that because it's going to be way over his head.' And then you see him extend that body and he catches it. It's an amazing thing."

Thus the basic dilemma that Coates presents to an opposing defense: Cover him with a big linebacker and he'll leave the guy in the dust; put a small, speedy safety on him and Coates will knock him aside like an inflatable doll.

"He's a tight end who's like an extra offensive lineman, and a tight end who's like an extra wide receiver," Bledsoe says.

The Patriots seemed to be taking Coates's versatility a step further when they lined him up at fullback to open a game in 1997. He was only a decoy on the play, but it got some people wondering what would happen if they gave the big guy a handoff.

"I guarantee you there would be no negative yardage," one teammate says, "and a lot of defensive linemen would be hurting after the play."

#87 BEN COATES, Tight End

YEAR	TEAM	NO	YDS	AVG	TD
1991	New England	10	95	9.5	1
1992	New England	20	171	8.6	3
1993	New England	53	659	12.4	8
1994	New England	96	1,174	12.2	7
1995	New England	84	915	10.9	6
1996	New England	62	682	11.0	9
1997	New England	66	737	11.2	8
1998	New England	67	668	10.0	6
CAREER TOTALS		458	5,101	11.1	48

Terrell Davis

Denver Broncos

It may go down as the most famous migraine headache in history. It happened to Terrell Davis before tens of millions of television viewers, and it very nearly changed the outcome of Super Bowl XXXII.

The Broncos were marching toward a go-ahead touchdown early in the game when Davis was sandwiched between Green Bay defenders Santana Dotson and LeRoy Butler after setting up first-and-goal at the Packers' 5-yard line. Davis had suffered from migraines since childhood, and he felt the familiar pain, observed the dreaded breakup of his visual field. And while he rested on the bench, then in the locker room, it was hugely apparent that Denver was a different team in his absence.

With Davis, the Broncos built a 14-7 lead; without him, they stalled, failing to gain a single first down and watching the Packers climb to within 17-14; with him again in the second half, they pulled out a memorable 31-24 victory. Davis's output—30 carries for 157 yards and a Super Bowl–record 3 rushing touchdowns—established him as the game's most valuable player.

The Packers had only themselves to blame. In 1995, as the NFL draft moved through the fifth round, Green Bay director of college scouting John Dorsey had suggested Davis, then a senior from Georgia. But he was overruled by general manager Ron Wolf. The Packers opted for The Citadel's Travis Jervey, leaving Davis to fall to the Broncos in the sixth round.

"I'd like to say it was great scouting," says Bob Ferguson, Denver's personnel director when Davis was drafted, "but if we'd known he'd turn out like he has, we would've picked him earlier. We weren't exactly geniuses."

In all, 19 running backs were drafted ahead of Davis that year. It seems absurd now that runners such as Ryan Christopherson, Corey Schlesinger, and Dino Philyaw would be drafted ahead of a future Super Bowl MVP, but nothing in

"You can't really arm-tackle him," Steelers linebacker Levon Kirkland says. "You have to kind of run through him."

Davis's background gave him the look of greatness.

He didn't play football until his junior year of high school; then he played six positions, including nose tackle. Davis went to Long Beach State to play for the one man who believed in him, George Allen. But Allen died a few months later, and Long Beach dropped its football program the next year. Davis transferred to Georgia but was hidden, first behind halfback Garrison Hearst, then behind the passing

of Eric Zeier. And when he did get chances, they often were cut short by injuries. He gained only 445 yards his senior year.

So it wasn't until his first NFL season that the world was able to appreciate what Terrell Davis brings to the game. You have to start with his strength. Though he is 5 feet 11 inches, 210 pounds, Davis runs like a much bigger man.

"When I am out there, I think I have a nose guard's or lineman's mentality," he says.

"You can't really arm-tackle him," Steelers linebacker Levon Kirkland says. "You have to kind of run through him."

And that's easier said than done because Davis has exceptional vision and cutting ability. Denver's rushing scheme is premised upon herding the defensive linemen outside, then having the runner cut upfield against the flow. Nobody does that better than Davis.

"He has great vision," Pittsburgh head coach Bill

Cowher says. "It just takes one guy not to get across the face of a block or one guy to be out of position, and he can hit a hole very quickly."

The quiet, self-effacing runner has proved to be such a perfect fit in Mike Shanahan's offense that his numbers are escalating at an astonishing rate. Davis went from 1,117 yards in 1995 to 1,538 in 1996 to 1,750 in 1997. He reached 4,000 yards in 41 games; only Eric Dickerson (33), Jim Brown (38), and Walter Payton (39) got there faster. He became the first Broncos rusher to post a 200-yard game when he pierced the Bengals for 215 yards on September 21, 1997; five weeks later he racked up 207 yards against the Bills. He also tied for the NFL lead with 15 rushing touchdowns in 1997.

But all that was just a hint of what was to come in 1998, when Davis became only the fourth player in NFL history (O.J. Simpson, Eric Dickerson, and Barry Sanders were the others) to rush for more

> "It's funny to me," Davis says of his NFL fortunes. "Sometimes I'm sitting at home, and I'll just laugh. If I'm dreaming, don't wake me up."

than 2,000 yards in a season. Davis averaged better than 5 yards per carry while amassing 2,008 yards. It was his first NFL rushing title. He also led the league with 21 rushing touchdowns and 23 total touchdowns.

More importantly, he helped the Broncos successfully defend their Super Bowl title. Denver's 34-19 victory over Atlanta in Super Bowl XXXIII made the Broncos the first AFC team to repeat as champions since the Steelers won XIII and XIV.

"He's the best back in football as far as I'm concerned, bar none," Denver quarterback John Elway said before he retired following the 1998 season. "He makes us such a balanced team."

When Davis helped Denver win Super Bowl XXXII, he did it about 15 minutes away from where he grew up in the gritty San Diego neighborhood of Lincoln Heights, which one police spokesman described as the poorest in the city. He originally had attended Morse High School, but saw himself turning into a delinquent.

"I even flunked PE," Davis says. "That's how bad it was."

So he transferred to Lincoln High, a small school best known as the training ground of Marcus Allen. A decade later Davis returned to Lincoln to have his old jersey (number 7) retired in a public ceremony. And five days after that he became the first Super Bowl MVP to win the award in his hometown.

"It's funny to me," Davis says of his NFL fortunes. "Sometimes I'm sitting at home, and I'll just laugh. If I'm dreaming, don't wake me up."

#30 TERRELL DAVIS, Running Back

| YEAR | TEAM | RUSHING | | | | RECEIVING | | | |
		NO	YDS	AVG	TD	NO	YDS	AVG	TD
1995	Denver	237	1,117	4.7	7	49	367	7.5	1
1996	Denver	345	1,538	4.5	13	36	310	8.6	2
1997	Denver	369	1,750	4.7	15	42	287	6.8	0
1998	Denver	392	2,008	5.1	21	25	217	8.7	2
CAREER TOTALS		1,343	6,413	4.8	56	152	1,181	7.8	5

Dermontti Dawson

We all know about NFL linemen. They snarl. They curse. They take candy from babies. Unless they are Steelers center Dermontti Dawson—in which case they bake cookies in their spare time and make plans to open a greeting card shop.

"He always has a smile on his face," Pittsburgh offensive line coach Kent Stephenson says. "He's one of those guys you know won't have an ulcer when he gets older. His attitude rubs off on all of us."

Dawson is so pleasant that his nickname in the Steelers' locker room is Ned Flanders, after the irrepressibly affable *Simpsons* character who is usually heard gushing, "Howdy, neighbor!"

"I have a big problem with players who talk, talk, and talk or push you around at the end of the play," says Dawson, who claims to have inherited his cheery nature from his Grandma Pauline. "I like players who concentrate on their own efforts."

Of course, when you're one of the best players in the NFL, you don't need to talk. "You can argue that a couple centers may be as good as Dermontti, but nobody is better," former Steelers guard Will Wolford says of his six-time Pro Bowl teammate. "That is a given."

When Dawson was playing guard at the University of Kentucky, his coach, Jerry Claiborne, used him as a one-man training film, running the projector and telling his other linemen, "This is how it's done."

At Pittsburgh, Dawson's speed allows the team

to run sweeps that most teams only can dream about. And at 6 feet 2 inches and 292 pounds, he more than holds his own in pass blocking.

"Sometimes I sit back and think, 'This guy is going to be in the Hall of Fame, and here I am next to him,'" Steelers guard Brendan Stai says. "It's a great honor."

The Pittsburgh fans might be less overwhelmed, but they have been spoiled by their snappers. Since 1964, the Steelers have had only three starting centers: Ray Mansfield, Mike Webster, and Dawson, who claimed the starting job in 1989. Mansfield played in a franchise-record 182 consecutive games; Webster is in the Hall of Fame. Dawson is more than worthy as a successor.

"Dermontti is a much better athlete than either Raymond or Mike," says former Steelers head coach Chuck Noll, who worked with all three. "Raymond was a heady player. He'd find a way to get the job done. Mike had great strength and power. Dermontti has it all—smarts, strength, quickness, and speed."

"I've never coached a center like him," adds Stephenson, who is in his thirty-fourth season of coaching. "He has outstanding quickness, which is a real key for the center position. He has unbelievable power and explosion.

"Dermontti is not a classic three-hundred-pound offensive lineman. There are people who are 'country strong' and people who are 'weight-room strong.' Dermontti is country strong."

Dawson grew up in Lexington, Kentucky, where he became a high school All-America in the shot put and discus. His family—including wife Regina and two children—lives in Lexington in the offseason, preferring the quiet, unglamorous life just as Dermontti prefers the anonymity of the offensive line.

Dawson's idea of success is to strap on a helmet and do his job every Sunday—and few are better at

> "Dermontti is not a classic three-hundred-pound offensive lineman. There are people who are 'country strong' and people who are 'weight-room strong.' Dermontti is country strong."
> — Kent Stephenson

it. Over the last 11 seasons, he has started 164 consecutive games. He is so dependable, in fact, that when he lay on the turf clutching his knee during a game against Baltimore in 1996, it was more than worrisome to his teammates. It was downright frightening.

"I almost had a heart attack," said Erric Pegram, who was a Steelers' running back at the time. "It was a horrible nightmare, like Amityville Horror, Jason, and Friday the Thirteenth all mixed up into one thing."

The nightmare ended three plays later when Dawson jogged back onto the field. He also hurt his head and his ribs that season, but he never left the lineup. So how does he do it? How does he avoid debilitating injury while those around him are fitted for casts and crutches?

"Just divine intervention and a little luck," Dawson says with a smile.

Brett Favre

Green Bay Packers

Brett Favre is the only player who could share the NFL most-valuable-player award and consider it a disappointment. Actually, Favre had nothing but good things to say about tying Detroit running back Barry Sanders for the most votes in 1997. But it was a slight backslide for the man who had won the 1995 and 1996 awards outright.

As it is, Favre is the only three-time winner of the *Associated Press* NFL MVP award. Denver's Terrell Davis was the 1998 MVP, but Favre probably will be fighting for the award again in 1999.

Any way you measure it, he is the yardstick for NFL dominance. You can begin with a throwing arm as strong as any in the league. His mother, Bonita, remembers a fifth-grade basketball game in which Brett launched a desperation heave the length of the court; it hit the far wall of the gym so hard that it knocked a fire extinguisher to the floor and broke it. At the NFL Quarterback Challenge in Hawaii one year, Favre launched a 79-yard pass—into a stiff breeze.

"He makes throws that other quarterbacks wouldn't dare," former Packers head coach Mike Holmgren says. "He can throw with terrific velocity even when he is in quite awkward positions."

But a strong arm will take an NFL quarterback only so far. Favre stands apart because he also hap-

pens to be one of the game's most intense competitors. It is a quality that naturally rubs off on his teammates.

"When you watch him play," says Packers general manager Ron Wolf, the man who got Favre in a 1992 trade with the Atlanta Falcons, "I don't think you ever have the feeling that his team is out of the game. It's like they'd always say about [Detroit's] Bobby Layne: He never lost a game; the clock just ran out on him."

Over the last four seasons, the clock hasn't run out on Favre very often. His Packers are 55-19 during that period, including a victory over the Patriots in Super Bowl XXXI. And always at the center of attention is the boyish passer with the Huck Finn freckles.

"In 1997, we saw [Buccaneers defensive tackle] Warren Sapp and Brett Favre jawing at each other in the playoffs," former NFL wide receiver James Lofton says. "Here was a quarterback who not only had the respect of his teammates, but also the respect of the most vaunted player on the other side. Sapp was admitting that the only way his team could win was not to shut

"Brett is one of the toughest guys on the team," wide receiver Robert Brooks says. "To know that your leader can endure punishment and not miss games—that he'll be there all the time—gives you a sense of confidence."

down the run or put on a strong rush, but to get inside the mind of Brett Favre and take him out of his game." It didn't work. It rarely does.

Mentally and physically, Favre is as rugged as a quarterback gets. Before his senior season at Southern Mississippi a car accident left him with a concussion, a cracked vertebra, and 30 fewer inches of intestine; five weeks later, he led the Golden Eagles to an upset victory at Alabama. He threw 5 touchdown passes against Chicago while playing with torn ankle ligaments in 1995, and he completed 23 of 33 passes with a separated left shoulder to help upset the Eagles in 1992. He entered the 1999 season

with 109 consecutive starts in regular-season games, far and away the most in the league.

"Brett is one of the toughest guys on the team," former Packers wide receiver Robert Brooks says. "To know that your leader can endure punishment and not miss games—that he'll be there all the time—gives you a sense of confidence."

It also helps when he's putting points on the board, and nobody does that better. He is the only NFL quarterback ever to log five consecutive 30-touchdown seasons. He had 39 scoring passes in 1996 and 38 in 1995, the third- and fourth-best season totals ever. After seven seasons in Green Bay, he owns club records for attempts (3,752), completions (2,318), and touchdown passes (213).

Favre seems to make everything look easy. In fact, about the only thing he finds difficult is dealing with celebrity. He sees himself as just an excitable country boy from Kiln, Mississippi, population 50. He still walks around with a stubbled chin, in a baggy sweatshirt. He still enjoys nothing more than fishing or playing golf. He can't help it if he happens to be one of the best athletes on the planet.

#4 BRETT FAVRE, Quarterback

YEAR	TEAM	ATT	COMP	PCT	YDS	TD	INT	RATING
1991	Atlanta	5	0	0.0	0	0	2	0.0
1992	Green Bay	471	302	64.1	3,227	18	13	85.3
1993	Green Bay	522	318	60.9	3,303	19	24	72.2
1994	Green Bay	582	363	62.4	3,882	33	14	90.7
1995	Green Bay	570	359	63.0	4,413	38	13	99.5
1996	Green Bay	543	325	59.9	3,899	39	13	95.8
1997	Green Bay	513	304	59.3	3,867	35	16	92.6
1998	Green Bay	551	347	63.0	4,212	31	23	87.8
CAREER TOTALS		3,757	2,318	61.7	26,803	213	118	89.0

Antonio Freeman

Injuries play a distinct role in football, as they do in any sport. For Antonio Freeman, they practically have steered his entire NFL career.

It was a career-ending neck injury to Sterling Sharpe that made the Green Bay Packers opt for help at wide receiver in the 1995 draft. They took Freeman in the third round. It was a major knee injury to Sharpe's heir, Robert Brooks, that made Freeman Brett Favre's go-to receiver in 1996. And, curiously, it was another injury—his own—that may have had the biggest impact on Freeman's career.

Just two weeks after Brooks's unfortunate episode, Freeman broke his left forearm chasing a pass over the middle. He would miss four games, while the Packers scrambled to find healthy bodies to play wide receiver. It wasn't until he got back onto the field (with a metal plate inserted in his arm) that Freeman realized what the interruption had done for his mental state.

"It sent me back out to play with a whole new attitude," he says. "You want to be the starting receiver all your life. I was the guy. Then all of a sudden, I get an injury. It gave me a chance to sit back and be critical of myself, and think about what I needed to do to be the best athlete I could possibly be."

Freeman must have unlocked some serious secrets, because he caught 25 passes for 452 yards and 4 touchdowns in December, sparking Green Bay's '96 playoff run. He hauled in an 81-yard touchdown pass against the Patriots in Super Bowl XXXI. It was the longest in Super Bowl

history, and it gave the Packers a lead they never relinquished.

That was the start of something huge for the previously unheralded receiver from Virginia Tech. His numbers continued to climb thereafter, culminating in a spectacular 1998 season that saw him catch 84 passes for a league-high 1,424 yards and 14 touchdowns.

Everyone knows of Freeman's exploits now, though they can't necessarily explain them.

"Some guys have more speed than he does," says Charlie Baggett, the Packers' receivers coach. "Some guys are bigger than he is. But he's a guy who you see consistently in the end zone. And I think that's the bottom line—the guy makes plays some kind of way."

One way is to run like heck after the catch, a Freeman specialty. "What impresses me is his ability to break tackles," Denver cornerback Ray Crockett says. "He's not a huge receiver like Herman Moore or

Cris Carter. And he never gets caught from behind."

Crockett should know. Though his Broncos emerged victorious, Freeman lit them up for 9 receptions, 126 yards and 2 touchdowns in Super Bowl XXXII. That was business as usual for a receiver who owns or is tied for 14 club postseason records after only four seasons. And remember, the Packers had their share of postseason glory under Vince Lombardi and Curly Lambeau.

> "One thing you realize is that you're going to get hit regardless of whether you catch it or drop it," Freeman says, "so you might as well make the best of it."

"The bigger the game, the better Antonio plays," Baggett says.

And the more intense the situation, the more the Packers look to number 86. "Antonio can get open down inside the twenty-yard line, where things are really happening," says Sherman Lewis, Green Bay's long-time offensive coordinator. "And with the guy we've got at quarterback [Favre], that ball is really coming at you. He zips it in there. The ball comes out of a bunch of arms and hands, but that's a catch Antonio can make. He has great concentration."

Such focus also comes in handy on crossing routes, the assignment that makes some receivers' limbs suddenly retract into their bodies. It was on such a route that Freeman broke his arm in 1996, but he has yet to shy away from hell-bent free safeties.

"One thing you realize is that you're going to get hit regardless of whether you catch it or drop it," Freeman says, "so you might as well make the best of it."

The man called "Free" credits an unlikely source with toughening him up for such painful work. It wasn't former Packers head coach Mike Holmgren, or hard-hitting teammate LeRoy Butler. It was Freeman's older brother Clarence, a staff sergeant in the U.S. Marine Corps.

"When we were back in college, Clarence would challenge my manhood," Antonio says. "He'd say, 'You're afraid to go across the middle. You're not tough.' And I always want to prove my big brother wrong."

So now those defensive backs know. The next time Freeman beats them for a tough grab in traffic, they can blame it all on Clarence.

#86 ANTONIO FREEMAN, Wide Receiver					
YEAR	TEAM	NO.	YDS.	AVG.	TD
1995	Green Bay	8	106	13.3	1
1996	Green Bay	56	933	16.7	9
1997	Green Bay	81	1,243	15.3	12
1998	Green Bay	84	1,424	17.0	14
CAREER TOTALS		229	3,706	16.2	36

Eddie George

Tennessee Titans

Sometimes, mother really does know best. If it weren't for Donna George's perceptiveness, who knows what would have become of her son, Eddie? It is highly unlikely he would have developed into a Pro Bowl running back.

Eddie George grew up in Philadelphia, which he describes as "hard-core and hard-nosed, a rough city, a blue-collar city." It was all of that for Eddie, and he wasn't helping matters with his attitude, or with the friends he kept.

"We'd do things like staying out late, drinking, gambling, and basically just being a menace to society," he says.

Donna had seen enough. She decided Eddie needed more structure in his life—and this was a unilateral decision. There was no debate, no show of hands. She helped him pack his bags, and off he went to Fork Union Military Academy in Virginia.

Fork Union was no picnic. It is a place where students have to rise at dawn, turn lights out by 10 P.M., and grunt through a lot of chores in between. It also happens to have a respected football program that already had produced Vinny Testaverde and Don Majkowski, a couple of future NFL quarterbacks.

"My mom sending me to the academy changed my attitude and my life," George says.

The rewards were not immediate, however. After an unspectacular senior season, George received no interest from the nation's college football programs. So he took matters into his own

hands. He found a directory of universities and made so many phone calls that his fingers hurt from punching buttons. The result? Zip. Not an offer.

George went back to Fork Union for a postgraduate year and rejoined the football team. He was declared ineligible after half a season, but that was all he needed to show his full package of skills. This time the college recruiters came out of the woodwork.

"I can't do what every man does," George says. "I have to do something extra."

George chose Ohio State, and in his freshman year he became one of the most recognizable players on the team. Unfortunately, it was because he fumbled twice at the goal line in a loss to Illinois. "I was the most hated person on campus," George says.

He had come too far to get bogged down by one game, though. George earned a starting role as a junior. And by the time he left Columbus he was

carrying the 1995 Heisman Trophy. He won the award after setting school records for rushing yards in a season (1,927) and a game (314 against Illinois), while scoring 25 touchdowns.

George's pace barely has slackened in the NFL. He ranked third in the AFC in each of his first three seasons, rushing for 1,368 yards in 1996, 1,399 in 1997, and 1,294 in 1998. They are the three most productive seasons in Titans' history for a running back not named Earl Campbell. He is one of only six players in NFL history to reach 4,000 yards in his first three seasons. It is the man at the top of that list to whom George most often is compared.

"He kind of reminds me of Eric Dickerson because he is big, strong, and powerful," Bills running back Thurman Thomas says.

A lot of 250-pound running backs are big and powerful. What puts the 6-foot 3-inch, 240-pound George in the category of Dickerson is his breakaway speed. "He can do both," agreed former Lions running back Barry Sanders. "He can cut and slash, and he can bruise you by running hard."

In his rookie season George broke a 76-yard run at Jacksonville, the club's longest in 13 years. Guys who weigh 232 pounds aren't supposed to do that. In the opening game of 1997, he cut, slashed, and bruised the Raiders for 216 yards, which tied Billy Cannon's franchise record.

George's exploits are the extension of his ceaseless drive. When a Titans' practice ends, it usually is just halftime for the muscled runner, who is known to put in an extra two to three hours of sweat. Most days he begins his post-practice workout with eight full-speed, 60-yard sprints, then heads to the weight room for a grueling workout.

"Eddie is a workhorse," Titans quarterback Steve McNair says. "That helps him be a better player because as the third and fourth quarter goes on and everyone else gets tired, he gets going."

That's one reason George labors so hard. A deeper explanation is that about eight years ago he started pushing himself as far as he could go, and now he doesn't know how to stop.

"I can't do what every man does," George says. "I have to do something extra."

#27 EDDIE GEORGE, Running Back

YEAR	TEAM	RUSHING				RECEIVING			
		NO	YDS	AVG	TD	NO	YDS	AVG	TD
1996	Houston	335	1,368	4.1	8	23	182	7.9	0
1997	Tennessee	357	1,399	3.9	6	7	44	6.3	1
1998	Tennessee	348	1,294	3.7	5	37	310	8.4	1
CAREER TOTALS		1,040	4,061	3.9	19	67	536	8.0	2

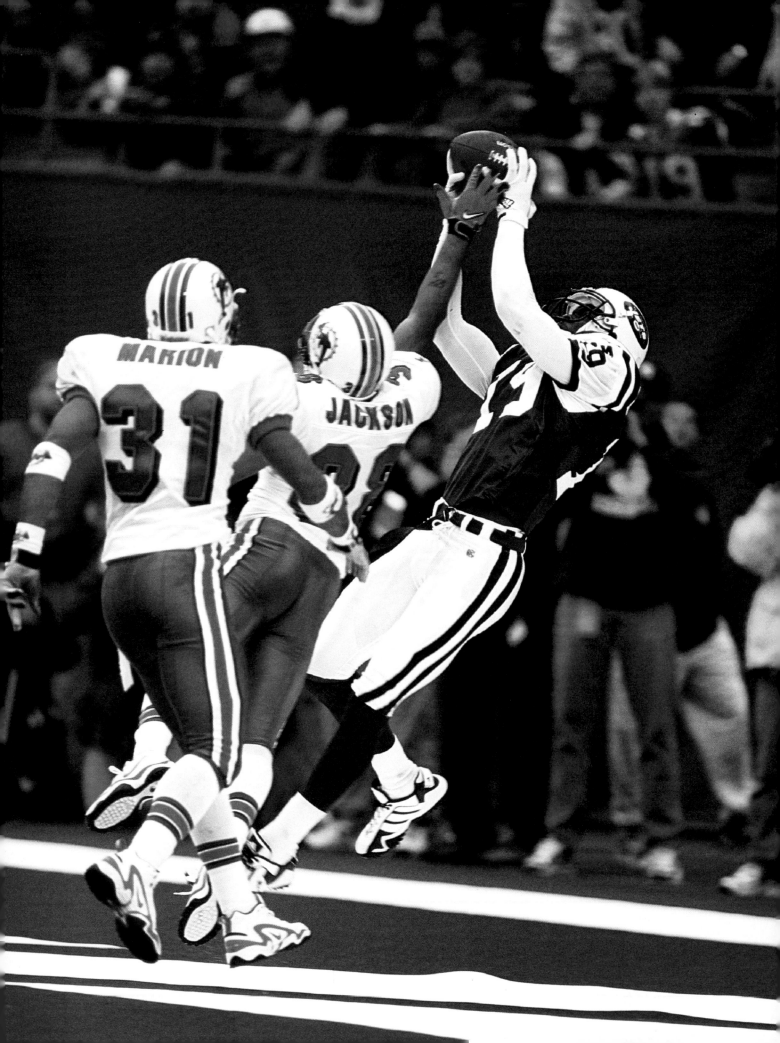

Keyshawn Johnson

New York Jets

Keyshawn Johnson is one of the few athletes who is renowned for his authorship as much as his athletic performance.

Not exactly a man of letters, Johnson wrote a 1997 autobiography that was more of the diss-and-tell variety. Even the title of the book—*Just Throw Me the Damn Ball*—was provocative. In it he criticized his head coach and demeaned a few of his fellow New York Jets, alienating him from teammates and fans alike. Don't wait for apologies.

"I shoot from the hip," Johnson says. "A lot of people live in a fictitious world. I speak reality."

To understand what drives Johnson into the glare of the spotlight, you have to examine his childhood. He grew up in south-central Los Angeles, in an area plagued by gangs. Two families, 17 people, shared his home. He never knew his father. Johnson had done time in two juvenile detention facilities by age 14. He wouldn't have escaped that environment without confidence.

He might not have done it without football, either. John Robinson, the famed USC coach, had a policy of opening his football practices to neighborhood youngsters. One of them was 7-year-old Keyshawn Johnson, who quickly became something of a team mascot. Future NFL greats such as Ronnie Lott and Marcus Allen took him out for Cokes after practice.

Johnson was the Trojans' ball boy for seven years; he was their offensive star for two. He caught 176 passes for 2,940 yards, setting a Pacific 10 Conference record with 102 receptions in 1995. He also led USC to New Year's Day victories in the Cotton Bowl and Rose Bowl.

It was this degree of success that encouraged the

Jets to make Johnson the first pick in the 1996 draft. And it was the same success that made Johnson so openly frustrated when New York went 1-15—the worst record in franchise history—in his rookie season.

The turnaround began a year later, when the Jets hired Bill Parcells as head coach. "For me, I thank God that I got Bill Parcells in my second year, because my first year was devastating," Johnson says. "At certain times I played well and at certain times I didn't play well. But ever since Parcells has been here, I think I have been very consistent in doing what the coaches have asked me to do."

Johnson improved steadily during his first three NFL seasons. A natural talent known for his ability to get off the line of scrimmage, and to hang on to the ball in traffic, he set about refining his game. He spent hours working on keeping his feet in bounds along the sidelines, hauling in countless passes from Jets assistant coach Todd Haley. He became a valuable downfield blocker.

"When he finds something he's struggling with," Jets offensive coordinator Charlie Weis says, "he's not leaving the field until he's got it corrected. There are a lot of football players who won't go the extra mile to be great. That's not part of his persona. He really wants to be the best receiver in the game."

By 1998 he wasn't far off the mark. With quarterback Vinny Testaverde firmly entrenched in the pocket, Johnson caught 83 passes for 1,131 yards and 10 touchdowns, earning his first Pro Bowl appearance. Only Isaac Bruce (224) caught more passes in his first three NFL seasons than Keyshawn's 216.

Johnson's varied skills were on vivid display in a '98 AFC playoff victory over Jacksonville. Not only did he catch 9 passes for 121 yards and 1 touchdown, he also scored another touchdown on a 10-yard reverse, ran 50 yards downfield to recover an important fumble, and intercepted a desperation pass by the Jaguars in the waning moments of the game.

"I am a team player," says Johnson, whose recent off-field endeavors include a major role in a motion picture and part-ownership in a restaurant in Beverly

> "My electricity can make everyone soar. I want to do it all and I can."

Hills. "But I am an individual first. I am going to shine. I know that I have electricity. My electricity can make everyone soar. I want to do it all and I can. And I have to be the number-one guy with the football, not number two or number three. It's like a company, a business—I can't be vice president. I've got to be president. That's who I am."

#19   KEYSHAWN JOHNSON, Wide Receiver

YEAR	TEAM	NO.	YDS.	AVG.	TD
1996	N.Y. Jets	63	844	13.4	8
1997	N.Y. Jets	70	963	13.8	5
1998	N.Y. Jets	83	1,131	13.6	10
CAREER TOTALS		216	2,938	13.6	23

Levon Kirkland

Pittsburgh Steelers

Somewhere in the bowels of Three Rivers Stadium there must be a top-secret laboratory that manufactures Pro Bowl linebackers. Because no matter how many the Steelers lose, they seem to be able to produce replacements.

First it was Hardy Nickerson, on the verge of stardom, who bolted to Tampa Bay as a free agent in 1993. In 1996, the Steelers were doubly depleted: pass rusher Kevin Greene signed with Carolina, then Greg Lloyd, one of the most intimidating players in the game, suffered a season-ending knee injury. That opened the door for young Chad Brown, but he, too, was gone a year later, to Seattle.

Yet the Pittsburgh defense has continued to thrive in the wake of the defections. And the biggest reason may be the guy with the biggest jersey number: 99, Levon Kirkland.

Kirkland has been to two Pro Bowls, and a play he made against Buffalo in 1996 suggests why. Driving in Steelers' territory, Bills quarterback Jim Kelly spotted tight end Lonnie Johnson breaking open over the middle. He lofted a pass, only to see Kirkland make a diving, over-the-shoulder, one-handed catch for an interception.

"Unbelievable play," Steelers director of team operations Tom Donahoe said afterward. "I thought he was beat. I'm sure Kelly did, too."

It was the kind of catch you would expect from Cris Carter or Herman Moore, not from a man built like a nose tackle. Kirkland stands 6 feet 1 inch and weighs 270 pounds, but it's hard to believe it when you see him move.

"He's a freak," Donahoe says. "It's not like you look at the guy and say he's heavy or fat. He's big,

thick, and can run. Physically he's awesome. He can just blow plays up."

"He does everything a receiver or a running back can do," Pittsburgh linebacker Earl Holmes says. "People think because he's big like that, he can't run. But we see it. He can run."

That's not the only way in which Kirkland's looks are deceptive. With his wire-rimmed spectacles and pensive gaze, the preacher's son from Lamar, South Carolina (the town of 1,300 where he still lives), appears to be a solemn man. Don't believe it. He reads comic books by the dozen, and he broke up the entire Steelers' locker room a couple years ago with an imitation of head coach Bill Cowher.

"I like to have fun," Kirkland says. "I like to cut up.

> "People think I'm serious. The only time I'm serious is when I play football."

If you look at me from a distance and did not know me, I'm wearing glasses and not smiling…I'm a big guy. People think I'm serious. The only time I'm serious is when I play football."

And then he is a serious problem for NFL offenses. Kirkland is one of those rare players who is both explosive and steady. On the one hand, he seems to have a knack for coming up big in crucial situations. In 1993, his first year as a starter, he preserved a 17-14 victory by stopping New England's Drew Bledsoe on a goal-line plunge. And there are many who feel Kirkland was the most valuable player of Super Bowl XXX. He roamed the field for 10 tackles, including a sack, but the Steelers came up short against Dallas.

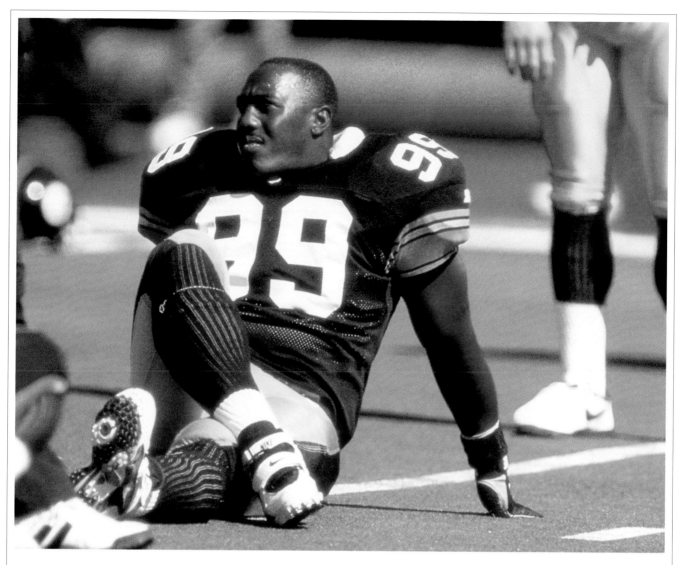

On the other hand, Kirkland consistently is effective. He hasn't missed a game in seven NFL seasons, and since moving into the starting lineup he has been the team's leading or second-leading tackler every year. He is a team captain (they call him Captain Kirk), and he calls the Steelers' defensive signals.

"He takes pride in getting people lined up, and has really assumed a leadership role in our defense," head coach Bill Cowher says. "His development has made him an integral part of what we do."

Kirkland still is adding new facets to his game. When Lloyd went down in 1996, Kirkland replaced him in Pittsburgh's Nickel and Dime packages. Lloyd returned in 1997, but by midseason Kirkland had regained his spot as a pass defender and wound up with a career-high 5 sacks while the defense improved markedly.

You might say he grew into the job, just as he grew into his body after going to Clemson as a 205-pound outside linebacker. It is said that Kirkland has played some games at 277 pounds. That might make him the largest linebacker ever to play in the NFL. Soon, he might be considered one of the best.

#99 LEVON KIRKLAND, Linebacker

YEAR	TEAM	TACKLES	SACKS	FUM REC	INT	YDS	AVG	TD
1992	Pittsburgh	5	0.0	0	0	0	—	0
1993	Pittsburgh	103	1.0	2	0	0	—	0
1994	Pittsburgh	100	3.0	0	2	0	0.0	0
1995	Pittsburgh	88	1.0	2	0	0	—	0
1996	Pittsburgh	113	4.0	0	4	12	3.0	0
1997	Pittsburgh	126	5.0	1	2	14	7.0	0
1998	Pittsburgh	137	2.5	0	1	1	1.0	0
CAREER TOTALS		672	16.5	5	9	27	3.0	0

Peyton Manning

Indianapolis Colts

A draft prospect's first meeting with an NFL team can be a rude introduction to the business of football. Young men recently lauded as campus heroes are suddenly picked apart, their tactical knowledge questioned, and their professionalism scrutinized. Peyton Manning's early pro contact was indeed an eye opener.

"I can still remember interviewing Peyton at the [scouting] combine," Bears vice president of pro personnel Mark Hatley says. "He came in, and he probably knew more about the Chicago Bears than I did. He asked questions about who we're going to put at this tackle, who we're going to get at guard, who we're going to get at wideout. I was just shocked."

Hatley should not have been so surprised. For anyone who has spent any time around Peyton Manning, the Indianapolis Colts young quarterback, knows he is slightly better prepared than your average Eagle Scout.

Perhaps it has to do with his upbringing. Peyton is the son of Archie Manning, the legendary quarterback who won glory at the University of Mississippi before a productive, if hard-knocked, pro career. Peyton and his brothers practically grew up in NFL locker rooms.

"After games we'd make tape balls," Peyton says, "and go out on the [Louisiana] Superdome field and toss those around."

Peyton would lie in his bed as a youngster, eyes closed, and listen to tapes of his dad's greatest college victories. He was already learning to break down film by the time he was in high school. Perhaps more than any other player in memory,

Peyton Manning was groomed for the National Football League.

"Sometimes I had the sense people were watching me closely, to see how I turned out," he says. "I think some of them would have liked to see Archie Manning's son mess up. I think it helped me be a better person, to think that someone was always watching me."

In setting eight NCAA records and building a 34-5 record as a starter during four years at the University of Tennessee, Peyton displayed a work ethic that bordered on the compul-

"From the first day, it was his huddle and his offense," Indianapolis tackle Adam Meadows says. "It might be cliché, but he acted like a ten-year veteran and had everyone's eyes on him."

sive. He organized informal passing drills in February, eventually bickering with the baseball coach over use of the field house. Meanwhile, he was taking enough units to graduate in three years with a major in speech communications and a minor in business. He spent so many nights holed up in his room with textbooks that his roommates called him Caveman. His grade-point average was 3.61.

Manning's diligence didn't end when the Colts selected him with the first pick in the 1998 draft. If anything, it grew.

Indianapolis quarterbacks coach Bruce Arians handed him a copy of the playbook on draft day; a few days later, at the team's first mini-camp, Manning was calling plays and making correct reads of the defense. He runs sprints after practice, throws during rest periods, and comes to the Colts' complex on Tuesday, the players' day off, for extra film study.

"Nobody watches more tape than Peyton," says Dom Anile, the Colts' director of football operations. "If it's a coverage that's been used somehow, somewhere in our league, he's seen it, and he understands it, and I guarantee he knows how to attack it."

Manning was the Colts' opening-day starter as a 1998 rookie, and he wound up as the only quarterback in the league to take every one of his team's offensive snaps. Along the way, he set NFL rookie records for attempts (575), completions (326), yards (3,739), and touchdown passes (26), ranking first or second in the AFC in each category—and this for a team run by Jim Mora, the notoriously conservative coach.

"From the first day, it was his huddle and his offense," Indianapolis tackle Adam Meadows says. "It might be cliché, but he acted like a ten-year veteran and had everyone's eyes on him. As far as I'm concerned, Peyton is the meal ticket."

And how does he compare with the old man? Veterans will tell you Archie was more mobile, a better all-around athlete, but that he couldn't match Peyton's size (6 feet 5 inches, 230 pounds) or arm strength. Colts fans are just hoping Peyton has better luck than Archie, who played for some of the worst teams in NFL history, though always with good-natured dignity.

"To tell the honest truth, I don't think I'll ever be as good a player as he was," Peyton says. "He was just great. But I can try to be the same person he was."

#18	PEYTON MANNING, Quarterback							
YEAR	TEAM	ATT.	COMP.	PCT.	YDS.	TD	INT.	RATING
1998	Indianapolis	575	326	56.7	3,739	26	28	71.2
CAREER TOTALS		575	326	56.7	3,739	26	28	71.2

Dan Marino

Miami Dolphins

When you talk about Dan Marino, the numbers start to fall like hail. During his 16-year NFL career, Marino has set so many major passing records that his write-up in the Miami Dolphins' media guide is longer than some pulp romance novels.

To begin with, Marino is the NFL's all-time leader in attempts (7,989 entering the 1999 season), completions (4,763), passing yards (58,913), and touchdown passes (408). He reached 30,000 yards, 40,000 yards, and 50,000 yards faster than any other quarterback. He has completed passes to 69 different players, from Mark Duper and Mark Clayton to Joe Rose, Irving Spikes, and even Dan Marino (after a pass was batted by an opponent). He has thrown touchdown passes to 50 different players—including 79 to former wide receiver Clayton—in 35 different stadiums. He is the only quarterback in NFL history to post six 4,000-yard seasons, and he set another mark in 1998 with his thirteenth 3,000-yard season.

He owns league records with 60 career 300-yard games and 21 games with 4 touchdown passes, and also had a record streak of 13 consecutive post-season games with a touchdown pass. He never has gone three consecutive games without a touchdown pass. In 1997, at a time when some claimed he had lost it, he set a Dolphins' record by throwing 156 consecutive passes with-out an interception while posting the NFL's sixth-highest passer rating. He has played in more regular-season games (231) in more seasons (18, including this year) than any other Miami player. In 1983, he set an NFL rookie record with a passer rating of 96.0, passing for 20 touchdowns with only 6 inteceptions.

"Nobody likes to have their records broken, but I'm very proud to have Danny break them," says Fran Tarkenton, who watched his major career marks tumble in 1995. "Nobody's played the game any better than Dan Marino. And I don't think, by the time he's done, that anybody will break those records in his lifetime."

Maybe by the time he's done we'll have figured out how he did it. Marino is big (6 feet 4 inches, 228 pounds), but some quarterbacks can throw the ball farther. He's never been much of a runner. And the Dolphins rarely have had a running game to support him.

But Len Dawson, the former NFL quarterback who now hosts a football show for HBO, has an

"Golfers get to play their sport just about their whole lives, baseball players play a pretty long time. But football, it's over fast, and once it's over you're not going to get that same feeling, the competition, Sunday afternoon."

explanation. "The one thing about Dan Marino that stands out, no matter what his physical condition might be, is his competitiveness," Dawson says. "He is one of those players who believes he's never out of it."

Most of the time he isn't. Marino's record as a starter is 142-87; without him the Dolphins are 8-10. Other observers point to his active mind for the game, and what might be the quickest throwing motion ever seen. As former teammate Jim Jensen says of Marino's delivery: "He sees it; it's gone. There's no thinking."

But that's too easy, according to Don Shula. "Everybody talks about Dan's quick release," says Shula, his coach for 13 seasons. "The

things that people don't talk about much are his abilities to make quick decisions and to sense when defenders are closing in on him."

Perhaps that is why the lumbering Marino has been sacked so few times in his career. In 1988, remarkably, he was sacked only 6 times while attempting 606 passes. And that, in turn, is part of why he has proved so durable. Despite numerous operations, Marino has suffered only one major injury: a torn Achilles tendon that knocked him out of 11 games in 1993 and still prevents him from rising up on his right toes without support. Before that setback he had started 145 consecutive games.

Marino was the last of the six quarterbacks chosen, the twenty-seventh pick overall, in the first round of the 1983 NFL draft, but he has outlasted all the others (John Elway was selected first by the Baltimore Colts before being traded to Denver, Todd Blackledge was taken seventh by Kansas City, Jim Kelly fourteenth by Buffalo, Tony Eason fifteenth by New England, and

> "Nobody likes to have their records broken, but I'm very proud to have Danny break them," says Fran Tarkenton.

Ken O'Brien twenty-fourth by the New York Jets).

His explanation for continuing is simple.

"I have a passion for playing the game," he says.

Besides, "Once it's gone, it's gone," he says. "You aren't coming back. Golfers get to play their sport just about their whole lives, baseball players play a pretty long time. But football, it's over fast, and once it's over you're not going to get that same feeling, the competition, Sunday afternoon."

Despite Marino's individual accolades, though, one feeling that has eluded him is that of a Super Bowl victory. He made it to Super Bowl XIX in only his second season, but lost to the 49ers and never has returned. As his career winds down, he now must face the possibility of leaving the sport without a championship. Believe it or not, he isn't all that worried about getting a ring.

"You've got to have dreams," Marino says. "But I can look back at my career knowing I worked for that goal each and every year, and I don't think it will take away from my career if I don't get one."

#13 DAN MARINO, Quarterback

YEAR	TEAM	ATT	COMP	PCT	YDS	TD	INT	RATING
1983	Miami	296	173	58.5	2,210	20	6	96.0
1984	Miami	564	362	64.2	5,084	48	17	108.9
1985	Miami	567	336	59.3	4,137	30	21	84.1
1986	Miami	623	378	60.7	4,746	44	23	92.5
1987	Miami	444	263	59.2	3,245	26	13	89.2
1988	Miami	606	354	58.4	4,434	28	23	80.8
1989	Miami	550	308	56.0	3,997	24	22	76.9
1990	Miami	531	306	57.6	3,563	21	11	82.6
1991	Miami	549	318	57.9	3,970	25	13	85.8
1992	Miami	554	330	59.6	4,116	24	16	85.1
1993	Miami	150	91	60.7	1,218	8	3	95.9
1994	Miami	615	385	62.6	4,453	30	17	89.2
1995	Miami	482	309	64.1	3,668	24	15	90.8
1996	Miami	373	221	59.2	2,795	17	9	87.8
1997	Miami	548	319	58.2	3,780	16	11	80.7
1998	Miami	537	310	57.7	3,497	23	15	80.0
CAREER TOTALS		7,989	4,763	59.6	58,913	408	235	87.3

Bruce Matthews

Tennessee Titans

As far as the Tennessee Titans are concerned, cloning technology is being refined a few decades too late. If only it were up and running now, Bruce Matthews might be the NFL's answer to Dolly the sheep. The Titans would love having five of him to open holes and protect the passer.

Matthews has started at all five offensive line positions during his career. We're not talking about token appearances, either. He has started 74 games at center (his current post), 67 games at right guard, 64 at left guard, 22 at right tackle, and 17 at left tackle—at least a full 16-game season at each. His 11 Pro Bowl selections include honors at all three interior positions. Matthews also is the team's long snapper for field goals and extra points.

"To have the ability to be flexible and dominate wherever you play is invaluable," New York Jets defensive coordinator Bill Belichick says. "What more could you ask of a player? Sell refreshments?"

Matthews would probably win Salesman of the Month. Versatility is nothing new to this guy. He was a prep All-America as both an offensive and defensive lineman at Arcadia High School in suburban Los Angeles. He also was a two-time all-league wrestler. At the University of Southern California, he filled all five offensive line spots at various times, earning consensus All-America honors at guard as a senior.

The Houston Oilers took him with the ninth pick in the 1983 draft, and Matthews has been starting ever since. One of his teammates in '83 was defensive end Elvin Bethea, who established club records by playing in 210 games over 16 seasons. Bethea passed the torch to Matthews, who broke the record by playing in 232 games by the

end of 1997. Matthews now is in his sixteenth season, too. His active run of 181 consecutive starts (entering 1999) is the longest streak in the NFL at any position—and he had to play through a painful knee injury in 1997 to keep it alive.

If the 6-foot 5-inch, 305-pound lineman's tenacity is hard to fathom, you must consider the values instilled by his father, Clay Matthews, Sr.

"I told all of them, 'You can go play any sport

you want to,'" Clay, Sr., says. "'But there are two rules. One of them is, I don't care if you're last string and sit on the bench all the time and you're the worst guy out there—you can't quit. Number two, if I ever see you play or practice and you're not giving it 120 percent of what you've got, I'm going to yank you out of there myself.'"

Dad wasn't barking empty words. His own determination allowed him to play four seasons as an end with the 49ers in the 1950s. And Bruce wasn't the only one listening. His older brother, Clay, Jr., played 19 seasons as a linebacker with the Browns and Falcons. They were teammates in two Pro Bowls.

Of the brothers, Bruce is probably dominant.

"Teams plan their defenses to stay away from [Bruce] Matthews," says Belichick, who believes the guard has been worthy of MVP consideration. "He is one of the few offensive linemen who can check the player in front of him and also pick up a blitzing cornerback or linebacker coming from the outside."

As Chargers linebacker Junior Seau says, "Matthews is going to know every move you make. Hopefully he'll make a false step, which he rarely does, and you can get by him."

Off the field, Matthews is just as steady. He holds a degree in industrial engineering. His favorite book is the Bible. He is a retiring man who relishes domestic life. "My entertainment and

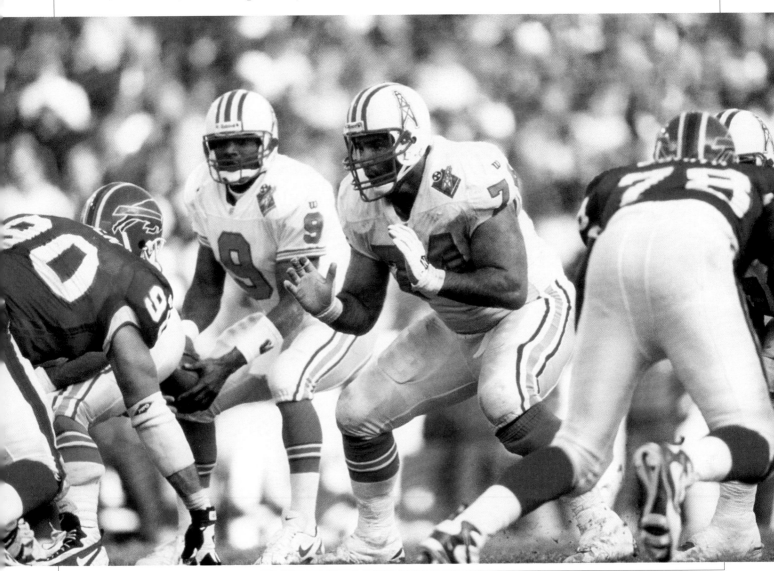

leisure time is spent playing with my four boys and girl [ages 5 to 14]," Matthews says. "Our existence is defined by our children."

That existence caught some minor turbulence when the franchise moved from Houston in 1997, just after the family had finished building a new home. Then again, change is not something that throws Bruce off balance. Besides all those position switches, he has powered offenses that ranged from the wide-open Run-and-Shoot to Tennessee's current attack, built around the hard running of Eddie George.

In an ever-changing game, it's helpful to have a few constants on which to rely. One of them is Bruce Matthews, still a pillar at age 38.

"I still feel like a kid," he says. "Then I look at the age and birth dates and realize that when I was in high school, a lot of these guys were being born."

Herman Moore

Detroit Lions

Herman Moore was destined to be a football star. He just had to experiment to find the right position.

His first try at George Washington High School in Danville, Virginia, was as a kicker. Moore actually set a school record with a 48-yard field goal, but his straight-on (non-soccer) style wouldn't have taken him very far. He caught a lot of passes as a senior, but mostly as a lanky tight end.

When Moore got to the University of Virginia, the coaches first tried him at defensive back. That experiment came to an end less than two weeks into preseason camp.

"I was playing free safety," Moore remembers, "and the fullback, Durwin Greggs, came through untouched. It was just me and him, and he ran me completely over. I reached to grab him and he never broke stride, just flattened me. That was my last play on defense."

As Moore lay on the turf, he probably wasn't dreaming about NFL stardom, but that is precisely what the future brought. After switching to offense and finding his position as a wide receiver, Moore set an NCAA record by catching touchdown passes in nine consecutive games as a junior. He joined the Lions as a first-round draft choice in 1991. He has maintained a similar pace in Detroit, and now holds club records for receptions (610 entering 1999), receiving yardage (8,467), and touchdown catches (57).

Moore is athletic and runs well after the catch, but he also is one of the best downfield blockers at his position. Already a head above the crowd of NFL defensive backs at 6 feet 3 inches, 210 pounds, he also is a great leaper. While his Virginia football teammates were enduring spring practice, Moore was winning both indoor and outdoor titles in the high jump. His best indoor leap, 7 feet 2 ½ inches, established a school record.

But conversations with his coaches and teammates usually turn to his hands. Though not exceptionally large, they are as powerful as vises. Moore does a lot of wrist curls, and grip work to keep his fingertips strong. One of his favorite exercises is taking an oval-shaped weight of one to three pounds and dropping it, then grabbing it before it hits the ground.

"I never learned to gather [the ball] in to my body," Moore says. "My security is catching it with my hands. If it's a play where I have to go low with my elbows on the ground, I'll still try to get my hands alone on the ball."

More often than not, he is successful. "With all due respect to the other fine receivers in this league," TV analyst and former linebacker Matt Millen says, "Herman Moore has the best pure hands of any of them. They're like Venus-flytraps. They just suck in those passes."

Moore's combination of height, hands, and leaping ability makes him the ultimate possession

> "With all due respect to the other fine receivers in this league, Herman Moore has the best pure hands of any of them. They're like Venus-flytraps. They just suck in those passes."
> — Matt Millen

receiver. Few players can reach as high; few balls escape his clutch.

He already had begun to show off his talents before 1995, but he joined the company of Jerry Rice and Michael Irvin in that breakthrough season. With Lions quarterback Scott Mitchell passing with regularity, Moore finished with an NFL-record 123 catches. His 1,686 yards were the fourth most in league history. And he hasn't slowed since. He finished second to Rice's 108 with 106 receptions in 1996 and tied Tim Brown for the NFL lead with 104 in 1997, becoming only the second player (Rice being the other) to register three consecutive

100-catch seasons. He had 82 receptions in 1998.

Don't expect the success to go to Moore's head. After signing a lucrative contract to begin his rookie NFL season, he and his wife Angela lived in a modest apartment and shared a pickup truck. When he showed up for his first preseason game, his wardrobe wasn't exactly from the Giorgio Armani collection.

"Man, did some of the other guys dog me!" Moore says. "I think the suit cost $129 at Sears. I had on $35 shoes."

Moore is one of Detroit's most popular athletes, a thoughtful, talkative guy who graduated with a bachelor's degree in rhetoric and communication studies. He also is a doting husband and father of two, and he and Angela are among the city's most visible spokespersons through Herman's Catch 84 Foundation.

"The attention I'm getting now means people might pay attention to some of the things I have to say," Moore says. "I talk to a lot of schools and community groups. We need people in the limelight to go out and get things across to young people, to help make things better for them."

#84	HERMAN MOORE, Wide Receiver				
YEAR	TEAM	NO	YDS	AVG	TD
1991	Detroit	11	135	12.3	0
1992	Detroit	51	966	18.9	4
1993	Detroit	61	935	15.3	6
1994	Detroit	72	1,173	16.3	11
1995	Detroit	123	1,686	13.7	14
1996	Detroit	106	1,296	12.2	9
1997	Detroit	104	1,293	12.4	8
1998	Detroit	82	983	12.0	5
CAREER TOTALS		610	8,467	13.9	57

Randy Moss

Minnesota Vikings

Bob Pruett tried to tell them, but they wouldn't listen.

Pruett, the head football coach at Marshall University, knew that the teams preparing for the 1998 NFL draft had concerns about Randy Moss's checkered past and his stone-faced demeanor. He attempted to set them straight.

"Randy has not had one single problem since he's been here at Marshall," Pruett said. "I don't think it's fair to keep chastising someone for as far back as his high school days. The team that gets Randy is going to get a whole lot better."

Many of the teams slotted in the first half of the first round were in dire need of help at receiver. But all of them passed on Moss. Finally, the Minnesota Vikings grabbed him with the twenty-first pick. And you know what? They got a whole lot better.

A decent 9-7 club the year before, the '98 Vikings went 15-1 and were one missed field goal away from reaching the Super Bowl. They also set an NFL record by scoring 556 points, an average of nearly 35 per game. And while Minnesota's offense was full of star power, it's clear that nobody made as much impact as the angular wide receiver from Rand, West Virginia.

"Randy Moss is six feet four, but he can do what a five-eight guy can do in terms of agility, quickness, and speed," says Hubbard Alexander, the Vikings' receivers coach. "His hands are as good as anybody's I've seen, and I know he can outjump just about anybody in the league. He's just a natural-born athlete."

Few would argue after witnessing Moss's scorching rookie season, in which he set an NFL rookie record with 17 touchdown receptions and was voted to a starting position in the Pro Bowl. Moss has height, leaping ability (39 inches), and daunting speed (sub-4.3 seconds in the 40-yard dash). Most of all, he has an innate ability to adjust to a ball in the air, something it takes most receivers years to perfect.

"If the ball is underthrown, Moss is going to go up and get it," says Doug Evans, the Panthers' veteran cornerback. "If it's overthrown, he can catch up to it with his speed."

At times it looked absurdly easy. "I remember looking over at Randy in the locker room and think-

> **"If the ball is underthrown, Moss is going to go up and get it," says Doug Evans, the Panthers' veteran cornerback. "If it's overthrown, he can catch up to it with his speed."**

ing, 'Jeez, this is like a scrimmage for this kid,'" says Brian Billick, the former Vikings offensive coordinator who now is head coach of the Baltimore Ravens.

Last season, the Vikings and Packers had a Monday night matchup at hallowed Lambeau Field, where Green Bay had not lost in 25 games. Moss proceeded to light up the defending NFC champions with 5 receptions for 190 yards and 2 long touchdowns, pacing the Vikings' 37-24 victory. Eight weeks later, on Thanksgiving Day, he burned the Cowboys at Texas Stadium, hauling in 3 scoring bombs of more than 50 yards each.

Even Dallas cornerback Deion Sanders was moved to remark, "I'm happy every time Randy Moss catches the ball, and every time a team that passed him up has to think about it."

Moss plays a position deep in talent. And though he caught an amazing 53 touchdown passes in two years at Marshall, the Thundering Herd didn't exactly face top-flight competition. But falling so far in the draft may have been a blessing for him. It allowed him to land in Minnesota, where head coach Dennis Green gave him a clean slate and his older brother, Eric, was on the roster as an offensive tackle. The Vikings also had Cris Carter, one of the most respected and learned receivers in the game, and he took Moss under his muscular wing.

"I want what's best for Randy," Carter says. "If it has to be at my expense—my catches, my touchdowns—that's all right. I sleep well at night knowing I never held him back from being a great player."

If anything, Carter has helped Moss reach his potential as a receiver. And as one division rival points out, that potential is abundant. "He's not the greatest receiver we ever faced," says Donnie Abraham, the Tampa Bay cornerback. "But he's going to be."

#84 RANDY MOSS, Wide Receiver

YEAR	TEAM	NO.	YDS.	AVG.	TD
1998	Minnesota	69	1,313	19.0	17
CAREER TOTALS		69	1,313	19.0	17

John Randle

Minnesota Vikings

Playing defensive tackle in the NFL is like slam-dancing in a pit full of grizzly bears. You are pummeled by offensive linemen, cut from the side by charging fullbacks, and sometimes nailed in the back by your own teammates. Most football players consider it the danger zone. But to Minnesota's John Randle, it's a piece of cake.

"In my life I've chopped cotton, picked watermelons, built fences, worked on an assembly line, worked in an oil field, built scaffolding," the five-time Pro Bowl defensive tackle says. "You know what? Those jobs are harder than football."

Randle grew up dirt-poor in the cotton fields of east Texas. For most of his childhood he was supported by a single mother who earned $23 a week as a maid. The family of four lived in a wood shack with a corrugated tin roof, an outhouse, and a bathtub that consisted of a bucket and a sponge. It was a hard life.

Certainly, there are guards and centers throughout the league who wring their hands and wish Randle had been raised as a spoiled rich kid because those humble roots have turned him into a monster on the football field.

"It makes me work," Randle says. "I want to give my family as much as I can. If it takes me working seven days a week to do it, I'll do it."

Randle's teammates call him "Motor," and he's usually revving pretty high. He used to tape sofa cushions to trees as a youngster, but he has replaced them with heavy bags like those used by boxers. He has been known to rope a log to his waist and run up

and down hills with it. "I had to tell the neighbors he wasn't crazy," his wife, Rosie, says.

"Going against him [in practice] is harder than going against anyone in the game," says guard Randall McDaniel, Randle's long-time teammate. "He doesn't know how to take breaks. You know he's coming full go, no matter if he's hurt, sick, whatever. He's coming a hundred percent every time."

Without that drive, it is unlikely Randle would have made it to the NFL. His older brother Ervin starred at Baylor before launching an eight-year career as an NFL linebacker. But John's SAT scores forced him to play at Trinity Valley Community College in Athens, Texas. He later transferred to Texas A&I, where he earned Little All-America honors as a senior, but that still placed him far from the spotlight. He was an undersized interior lineman (Randle is 6 feet 1 inch, 283 pounds now, but he weighed much less at the time) from a small school, and he went unclaimed in the 1990 draft.

As Randle remembers, "It was then that I told God, 'If you just give me one chance, I'll never look back and say, "What if?"'"

Randle got his chance, and he was starting for Minnesota by his second season. He was voted to his first Pro Bowl in 1993, but he soon found key teammates (such as Pro Bowl defensive tackle Henry Thomas) and coaches (such as defensive coordinator Tony Dungy) moving on. So Randle picked up any slack that had existed in his routine.

He got into even better shape and refined his

"He doesn't know how to take breaks. You know he's coming full go, no matter if he's hurt, sick, whatever. He's coming a hundred percent every time."
— Randall McDaniel

already-nifty moves. He also became an amateur detective, looking into his opponents' backgrounds to tailor his distracting on-field chatter. Enemy quarterbacks constantly tell their blockers not to listen to Randle, but by the fourth quarter the mile-a-minute talker usually has them distracted and frustrated.

As if he needed the extra advantage. Since 1991, Randle has more sacks (95) than any other player in the NFL. In 1997, he led the league with 15½. That accomplishment goes from impressive to unbelievable when you consider that he plays in the middle, where he rarely gets an open route to the quarterback.

"John is the toughest player I play," Green Bay's Brett Favre says. "On artificial turf he's unblockable."

Noting Randle's exemplary effort and high-octane performance, the Vikings made him (briefly) the highest paid defensive player in the history of the NFL in February, 1998.

"There is only one John Randle," former Minnesota vice president Jeff Diamond said at the time. "If there is a player worthy of this type of contract, it is John. He is the heart and soul of our defense."

Randle's rags-to-riches story was complete.

#93 JOHN RANDLE, Defensive Tackle

YEAR	TEAM	TACKLES	SACKS	FUM REC	INT	YDS	AVG	TD
1990	Minnesota	21	1.0	0	0	0	—	0
1991	Minnesota	58	9.5	0	0	0	—	0
1992	Minnesota	56	11.5	1	0	0	—	0
1993	Minnesota	59	12.5	0	0	0	—	0
1994	Minnesota	47	13.5	2	0	0	—	0
1995	Minnesota	47	10.5	0	0	0	—	0
1996	Minnesota	58	11.5	0	0	0	—	0
1997	Minnesota	71	15.5	2	0	0	—	0
1998	Minnesota	56	10.5	1	0	0	—	0
CAREER TOTALS		473	96.0	6	0	0	—	0

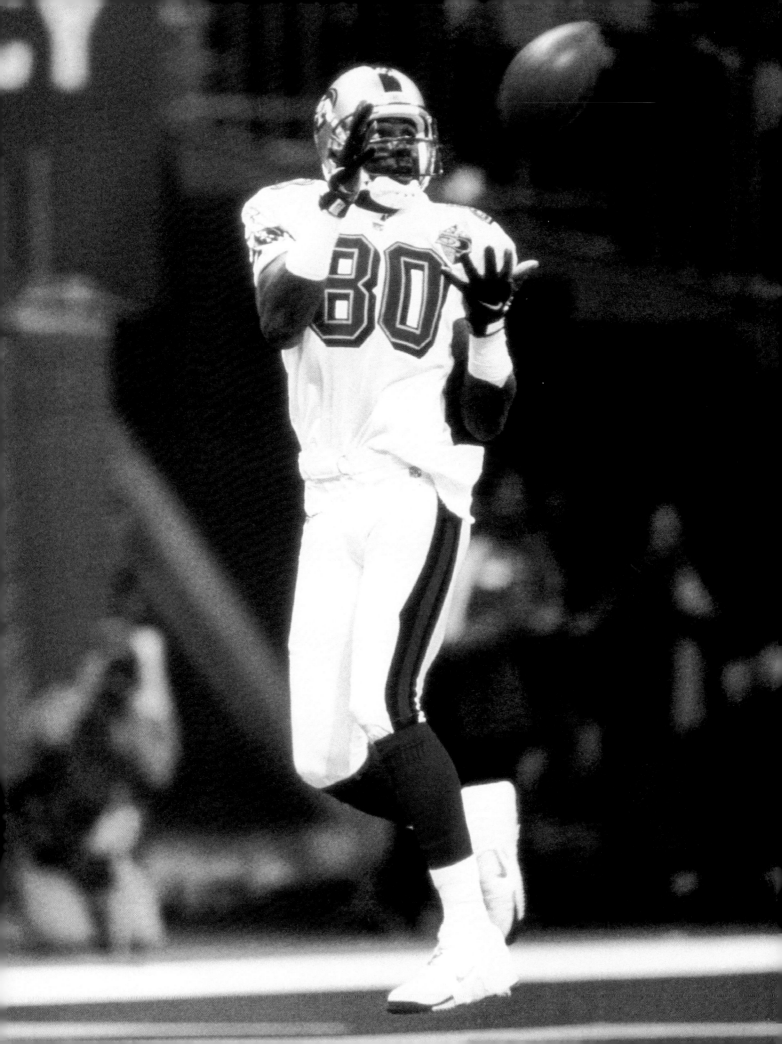

Jerry Rice

San Francisco 49ers

When Jerry Rice was in junior high school in tiny Crawford, Mississippi, he decided to cut school one day. The principal saw him and gave chase. Impressed with the boy's speed, the administrator (after catching him and spanking him thoroughly) directed him to the football coach.

That principal, his name forgotten, has been cursed by a generation of NFL defensive backs. Without his meddling, they figure, maybe Rice would have become, say, an electrician.

Football fans used to argue about whether Rice was the best wide receiver of his day. Then he started setting records—most touchdowns in a season (22 in 1987…in only 12 games!), most touchdowns in a Super Bowl (3, twice), most career catches in the postseason (124). Then folks started debating who was the greatest receiver of all time, Rice or Don Hutson. And Rice set more records—most career receptions, receiving yardage, and touchdowns, most receiving yards in a season (1,848 in 1995), etc., etc. Now, the only question is whether Rice is the greatest NFL player ever, at any position.

Few who have played with or against him would vote otherwise.

Wymon Henderson wouldn't—not after a particular reception Rice made against him in 1993.

"I never even saw the catch,"

Henderson, then a Rams' cornerback, said afterward. "I had one of his arms. I had him pinned. I didn't think it was possible for him to catch the ball. When I saw him still running, I thought, 'How in the world did he catch the pass?'"

It's a question that has been asked often. Rice is 6 feet 2 inches, 196 pounds, relatively average by NFL standards. He is not a Jordanesque leaper, and his speed is surpassed by many other receivers—during time trials, anyway. As former 49ers safety Ronnie Lott once said, "Jerry has four-six speed on Tuesday and four-two

"I think he believes that if they covered him with eleven guys," Young says, "he should still be open and win the game."

speed on Sunday. Nobody outruns him in a game."

That's the thing: On Sundays, no one is better than Rice.

"He's the talent you look for to define all the skills," says R.C. Owens, the former 49ers receiver who is an executive assistant with the club. "He runs the field, pattern-wise, with great precision. He

gets off the line. He has three speeds, and changes them at any time. He has great hands. He can react to the ball wherever it is."

What sets Rice apart from other pass-catchers—and apart from the cornerbacks who are trying to stay with him—is devotion to his craft. He used to get equipment manager Ted Walsh, a left-hander, to warm him up for lefty quarterback Steve Young's passes. The fluid patterns Rice runs, the ones that look so effortless, are the product of countless, tedious hours spent working on routes before and after regular practice.

"I think he believes that if they covered him with eleven guys," Young says, "he should still be open and win the game."

Rice's running form was perfected by numerous sessions with a personal trainer, who helped him limit the bounce in his stride. His footwork was refined by jumping rope. And his physical stamina—which might compare favorably to a distance runner's—is equally manufactured. As soon as each season ends, Rice starts on his conditioning. His daily wind-sprint regimen usually starts with "accelerators": gain speed for 20 yards, sprint at full throttle for 60, decelerate for 20, then turn around and immediately do it 13 more times.

"I think it would blow people away to know how hard Jerry works during the week," retired tight end Brent Jones says. "And I'm talking about people on other teams, not the fans. Jerry runs hard—every play, every day."

He ran hard while setting 18 NCAA Division II records at Mississippi Valley State, and he ran hard when the 49ers traded up to take him in the first round in 1985. Since then, Rice has spanned the gaps of 49ers greatness. Among others, he has caught passes from Joe Montana and Steve Young, taken orders from Bill Walsh and George Seifert, run plays called by Mike Holmgren and Mike Shanahan.

Rice played 188 games over 12 seasons without missing one. Then the unthinkable happened. He suffered a major knee injury in the first game of 1997, made an amazing recovery to return for the next-to-last game, then hurt a different part of the knee.

Fans worried that the injuries might induce Rice to retire. The opposite is true.

"[I learned] how much I loved this game," says Rice, who returned to catch 82 passes in 1998. "The fire's still inside. [This injury] was meant to happen, to make me realize what football means to me."

And what Jerry Rice means to us.

#80 JERRY RICE, Wide Receiver

YEAR	TEAM	NO	YDS	AVG	TD
1985	San Francisco	49	927	18.9	3
1986	San Francisco	86	1,570	18.3	15
1987	San Francisco	65	1,078	16.6	22
1988	San Francisco	64	1,306	20.4	9
1989	San Francisco	82	1,483	18.1	17
1990	San Francisco	100	1,502	15.0	13
1991	San Francisco	80	1,206	15.1	14
1992	San Francisco	84	1,201	14.3	10
1993	San Francisco	98	1,503	15.3	15
1994	San Francisco	112	1,499	13.4	13
1995	San Francisco	122	1,848	15.2	15
1996	San Francisco	108	1,254	11.6	8
1997	San Francisco	7	78	11.1	1
1998	San Francisco	82	1,157	14.1	9
CAREER TOTALS		1,139	17,612	15.5	164

Darrell Russell

Oakland had been duped again. Everyone said so. The Raiders had traded up for the second pick in the 1997 NFL draft, and it was no secret they desperately needed help on the offensive line. So they must have been after Orlando Pace, the mountainous tackle from Ohio State, right?

The St. Louis Rams thought so. They offered an even richer package to the Jets and came away with the number-one choice, which they used to snatch Pace. The Raiders took USC defensive lineman Darrell Russell with the next pick and claimed he was the guy they had coveted all along.

Two-and-a-half years later, it isn't so crazy to think Oakland valued Russell more highly than his more glorified counterpart. Pace still is considered a potential superstar, but has been somewhat prone to injury. And Russell might be the best young defensive tackle in the league.

"Darrell's quick, but he's big and strong, too," says Willie Shaw, the Raiders' defensive coordinator. "He's been absolutely great in his position."

Of course, settling on that position has been the key. During his '97 rookie season, Russell played mostly at defensive end, not his natural position in college or high school. He performed adequately (43 tackles, $3\frac{1}{2}$ sacks), but seemed unable to break out of the pack.

Then Shaw arrived, hired away from the Saints. He scrapped the Raiders' read-and-react defense and instituted his own model, an aggressive scheme that sends the linemen immediately into the gaps. And he wasted no time in moving Russell inside.

"End was not his cup of tea," Shaw says. "He was too wide. He looked lost in space sometimes."

The change yielded striking results for the Raiders. The defense, which had finished last in the NFL in yards allowed the previous year, became one of the league's most formidable. There were many important contributors, including the new cornerback tandem of Charles Woodson and Eric Allen. But none of it could have happened without the fearsome Russell, who had 10 sacks and nearly constant penetration.

In effect, he became Shaw's ace in the hole. "On certain plays we try to get him a little wider, let him

"I never really had a father figure around," Russell says. "I didn't search for one because I had my mom. That's all I needed."

jet hard up the field," Shaw says. "He's usually quicker than the guard across from him, but just as big. A lot of times the guard can't get out on him in time. And if we see a situation where they put someone quick in front of Darrell, we'll say, 'Okay, just railroad him.' It depends on the game plan, and it depends on the guard."

As influential as Shaw has been, he is not the person given the highest degree of credit for getting Russell on a fast path to success. That honor falls to Darrell's mom, Eleanor.

"I never really had a father figure around," Russell says. "I didn't search for one because I had my mom. That's all I needed."

Darrell's parents divorced when he was 5. His father moved from San Diego to the East Coast, and Eleanor poured her soul into raising the child. Her commitment was consistent. For example, she didn't want to seem hypocritical when preaching against alcohol and drugs, so she didn't have a single drink—not a beer or even a small glass of wine—during Darrell's adolescence.

Everything took a back seat to Eleanor's boy, including her social life. "If there were any conflicts between Darrell and someone I dated, the guy had to go," she says. "Some of my friends said I went overboard."

Eleanor punched a time clock as a factory worker, then as a computer programmer. The Russells weren't rich, not by a long shot, but she stashed enough money to send Darrell to private schools, including respected St. Augustine High School, where he was the San Diego Section defensive player of the year as a senior.

"I can't really put my appreciation for her into words," Darrell says. "I can't fathom putting your whole life on hold the way she did for me."

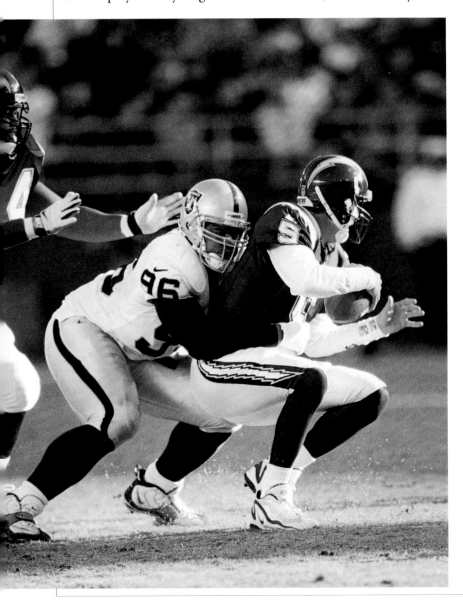

There are many lessons to be learned from a hard-scrabble childhood. The Russells never had much of a cash surplus, so when something in the house broke, Darrell learned to fix it. One example: He replaced a leaky kitchen sink when he was 11. Along the way, he also got pretty good at plugging holes on the line of scrimmage.

#96 DARRELL RUSSELL, Defensive Tackle

YEAR	TEAM	TACKLES	SACKS	FUM. REC.	INT.	YDS.	AVG.	TD
1997	Oakland	43	3.5	0	0	0	—	0
1998	Oakland	63	10.0	1	0	0	—	0
CAREER TOTALS		106	13.5	1	0	0	—	0

Deion Sanders

Dallas Cowboys

In his NFL debut with Atlanta in 1989, Deion Sanders returned his first punt 68 yards for a touchdown. Five days earlier he had blasted a home run for the New York Yankees. Just like that, Sanders became the only athlete to score an NFL touchdown and hit a major league home run in the same week.

Welcome to Prime Time.

In the ensuing years, a nation of sports fans would come to believe there was nothing Sanders could not do, no envelope he couldn't stretch. In January, 1995, he became the first man ever to play in both a World Series (he hit .533 for the Braves in 1992) and a Super Bowl (he intercepted a pass for the 49ers in game XXIX; a year later, he would catch a 47-yard pass for the Cowboys in game XXX). In 1996, he became the first NFL player in 36 years to start on both offense and defense in the same season. In 1998, he recorded his seventeenth touchdown return. For those keeping score, that's 8 interceptions, 5 punt returns, 3 kickoff returns, and 1 fumble recovery, all ending in paydirt. Of course, that doesn't count his 3 touchdown catches or the time he scored on a reverse against Philadelphia in the 1995 playoffs.

But Sanders's unique versatility sometimes obscures the fact that he does one particular thing—covering wide receivers—as well as anyone else who ever has played the game. "Deion is the first player to be able to dominate and dictate a game from the defensive back position," commentator John Madden says.

"He takes one-third to one-half of the field away from the offense," former receiver Willie (Flipper) Anderson explains. "He'll be playing man-for-man on one guy, and the rest of the secondary will be playing zone. The quarterback is afraid to throw at Deion, and that frees the safety to cheat over to the opposite side."

What makes Sanders so formidable? His surprising upper-body strength (he's rather slender at 6 feet 1 inch, 195 pounds) helps him jam receivers at the line. He can stop and

> "He studies and he studies. He knows his opponent inside-out long before he steps out on to the field to play."
> — Tom Holmoe

start on a dime, and he has the strong hands of a baseball player. But above all is that supernatural speed.

"If you throw the ball out there and your receiver has a step, it shouldn't matter how quick he is," says long-time NFL quarterback Wade Wilson. "Well, it matters in Deion's case. He would lay low, and when the receiver went by him, he made up the ground while the ball was still in the air. I've never seen anybody who has been able to do that. It's phenomenal, but he

can actually catch up to the ball. He's that fast."

Sanders is a natural athlete. He once played a baseball game for Florida State, went over to the campus track and ran a leg of the 4x100-meter relay (in his baseball pants), then jogged back to the diamond and slapped the game-winning hit in the Seminoles' second game. In 1997, after finishing second in the National League with 56 stolen bases for the Reds, he reported to the Cowboys' camp on August 27. He took part in two days of

meetings and one noncontact practice, and started the season opener on August 31.

But don't be fooled. Sanders also is one of the hardest-working athletes you'll ever see. He rides his bicycle 5 to 12 miles most offseason mornings, and often plays basketball after practice. And he breaks down film like a scientist.

"Deion knows a tremendous amount about football," says Tom Holmoe, his former position coach in San Francisco. "He studies and he studies. He knows his opponent inside-out long before he steps out on to the field to play."

The image of the devoted student is far from Sanders's public picture. He wears $5,000 teal suits and more gold than an Egyptian pharaoh. He cut an album called *Prime Time*, with a single, "Must Be the Money," that hit the Top 10 on the R&B charts. He is not hesitant to boast of his abilities, or of his bank account. But teammates insist there is more to the man than meets the eye.

"These are things ya'll don't know about Deion because it doesn't get publicized," former Cowboys guard Nate Newton says. "He doesn't drink. He doesn't do drugs. He doesn't cuss. He's a strong family man. He's only flashy when he's out in the public entertaining."

And he's never flashier, never more entertaining, than when he's running stride-for-stride with the NFL's best receivers, hoping a quarterback will buck the odds and throw the ball his way.

#21 DEION SANDERS, Cornerback

YEAR	TEAM	TACKLES	SACKS	FUM REC	INT	YDS	AVG	TD
1989	Atlanta	39	0.0	0	5	52	10.4	0
1990	Atlanta	50	0.0	0	3	153	51.0	2
1991	Atlanta	49	1.0	0	6	119	19.8	1
1992	Atlanta	66	0.0	1	3	105	35.0	0
1993	Atlanta	34	0.0	0	7	91	13.0	0
1994	San Francisco	37	0.0	0	6	303	50.5	3
1995	Dallas	28	0.0	0	2	34	17.0	0
1996	Dallas	45	0.0	3	2	3	1.5	0
1997	Dallas	29	0.0	0	2	81	40.5	1
1998	Dallas	28	0.0	0	5	153	30.6	1
CAREER TOTALS		405	1.0	4	41	1,094	26.7	8

Warren Sapp

Warren Sapp made the Pro Bowl in 1998, and his Tampa Bay Buccaneers won four of their last five games to finish 8-8. So you think Sapp was a happy man?

"I hated seeing the films," the blunt defensive tackle says. "You know what it's like when your mother puts something on your plate that you hate, and you know you have to eat it? That's what it was like. I would go home Sunday night, and I knew I played terrible. The next morning I'd get up, and I'd have to go eat that asparagus."

The problem was that Sapp had swallowed a lot more than asparagus during the previous offseason. He had been the toast of the NFL in 1997, recording $10\frac{1}{2}$ sacks and generally terrorizing opposing offenses from start to finish. He got married while in Hawaii for the Pro Bowl, then was rewarded with a generous six-year contract. Life was good, and the big man came to camp looking pampered.

"I was fat," says Sapp, never one to mince words. "No two ways to say it. I was just too fat. I couldn't go sixty plays without a rest."

He was still better than most pass rushers in '98. He just wasn't good enough.

"If I play on an okay level, we're going to be all right," Sapp says. "But when I'm playing my game the way I play it and everybody is feeding off each other, we're something special. And that's what you have to be in this league to win a championship."

Sapp rededicated himself to success. He hired a personal nutritionist and shed nearly 40 pounds

during the '99 offseason. "No meals after seven o'clock," he says. "That's a killer, telling a three-hundred-pound man he can't eat after seven o'clock. But that's the commitment I made to myself, to get myself into shape to help this ball club win more games."

Sapp showed up looking more fearsome than ever in 1999, and the Buccaneers' defense quickly reverted to form. Tampa Bay allowed just 4 first downs and 107 total yards in the season opener against the Giants. Against Philadelphia a week later, Sapp came through with 3 sacks.

"This guy is a one-man wrecking crew," Denver guard Mark Schlereth says. "You watch him on film, and he's a freak of nature. He's unbelievable. Nobody's blocked him yet."

That set up a meeting with the Broncos and a possible matchup with young guard Chris Banks, who had played in only four NFL games. A reporter asked Denver's Mike Shanahan how Banks would feel lining up against Sapp, and the coach replied, "How would you feel about going one-on-one with the best sportswriter in America?"

Sapp was back, a fact that sent a shudder through the locker rooms of the NFL.

"This guy is a one-man wrecking crew," Denver guard Mark Schlereth says. "You watch him on film, and he's

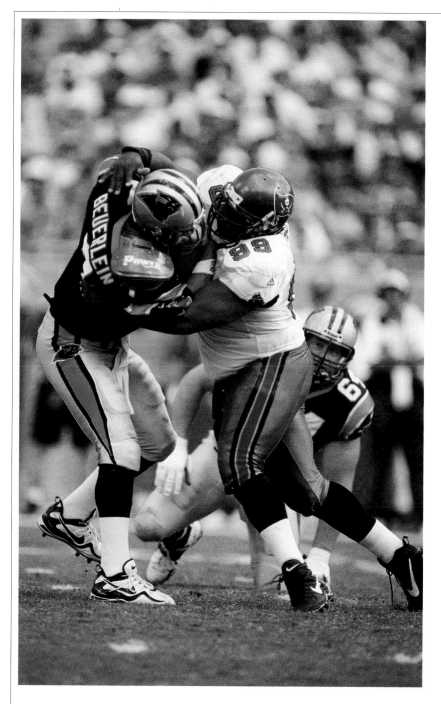

He refers to opposing quarterbacks as "the hunted" and "fresh meat."

"They all smell like chicken, which is my favorite food," he says with a laugh.

Sapp doesn't try to contain his personality. As a youngster, he got report cards praising his school-work but advising him to keep quiet. It's much the same now. He spent much of a '97 playoff game facemask-to-facemask with Green Bay quarterback Brett Favre, and he's jawed at just about every other passer in the league.

"If I can talk to them and maybe get their minds off looking at the receiver down the field—maybe focus in on me and where the rush is coming from," Sapp says, "I am helping my ball club."

And make no mistake, the Buccaneers are Sapp's team. They soak up his energy and follow his lead. "There are stars and extras," says Tony Dungy, Tampa Bay's cerebral head coach. "You hate to look at it like that, but it's true. Movies aren't great because the extras are great. They're great because Tom Cruise is great.

"On this team, Warren is Tom Cruise."

And when they play Tampa Bay, a lot of NFL quarterbacks keep their eyes wide shut.

unbelievable. Nobody's blocked him yet."

There is no way Sapp should be able to juke seasoned offensive linemen, but he does. His build—nearly 300 pounds packed onto a rounded 6-foot 2-inch frame—belies tremendous athletic ability. Sapp scored 1,000 points as a high-school basketball player, including 42 in one game (he nailed a three-pointer to break 40). And he was recruited to the University of Miami as a tight end.

That seems like a clear case of miscasting because Sapp definitely has a defender's mentality.

#99 WARREN SAPP, Defensive Tackle								
YEAR	TEAM	TACKLES	SACKS	FUM REC	INT	YDS	AVG	TD
1995	Tampa Bay	27	3.0	0	1	5	5.0	1
1996	Tampa Bay	51	9.0	1	0	0	—	0
1997	Tampa Bay	68	10.5	1	0	0	—	0
1998	Tampa Bay	59	7.0	1	0	0	—	0
CAREER TOTALS		205	29.5	3	1	5	5.0	1

Junior Seau

San Diego Chargers

When Junior Seau was a senior at Oceanside High School in southern California, he met then-Chargers quarterback Dan Fouts at a local function. Fouts knew that Seau was a two-position star, and he asked the young athlete whether he would be playing tight end or linebacker at USC.

"I'm not sure," Seau replied.

"Play linebacker," Fouts advised. "They make more money."

It was a wise audible by the quarterback. Twelve years later, Seau signed a six-year, $27.1 million contract extension with the Chargers that made him, at the time, the highest-paid linebacker in the history of the sport.

Seau was thrilled about the cash, to be sure, but the deal meant more to him. "This is more of a contract to make sure I'm home and performing in front of the people who watched me grow," he said at a press conference.

Seau is the essence of a hometown hero, an affably bombastic football star who owns a highly visible hip-hop clothing line (Say Ow! Gear) and San Diego's most popular sports establishment (Seau's, The Restaurant). But part of the reason he is so popular in California's southern extreme is not because of what he has, but because of what he has given to get there.

Tiaina Seau, Jr., split his early life between Oceanside, a working-class community with strong military ties, and American Samoa, his ethnic homeland. He didn't speak English until he was 7. He lived in a poor neighborhood, in a house

so full of relatives he slept between the washing machine and the mop in the family garage.

But it was clear early on that Seau's physical gifts were vast. After achieving All-America status at USC, Seau went to the Chargers in the first round of the 1990 draft, making him the first selection of the Bobby Beathard era in San Diego.

Soon he was the most popular player on the team.

It's hard not to be won over by someone who plies his trade with such intensity. Seau plays every game, every snap, as if his life depends on it. Teammates call him the Tasmanian Devil. His trademark "Lightning Bolt" dance makes him the target of opposing fans' outrage, but it's a crowd pleaser at Qualcomm Stadium.

"With Junior, it's spontaneous," says Bobby Ross, his former head coach. "He makes a lot of money, but he'd probably play for free. I know it's true because he practices pretty much the same way."

Seau constantly pushes himself to improve. He spends about 10 hours a week in the weight room during the offseason, further chiseling one of sport's most unbelievable bodies. He can bench press nearly 500 pounds and curl 170-pound dumbbells. And yet he can run the 40-yard dash in 4.61 seconds.

"If I had a hundred-thousand dollars," former Chargers defensive end Burt Grossman once said, "I'd train Junior and have him lose twenty pounds, then put him in the decathlon. I'd put him up against Dan [O'Brien] and Dave [Johnson]—together. There's nothing he can't do athletically."

Such a work ethic has allowed Seau to improve

> "With Junior, it's spontaneous," says Bobby Ross, his former head coach. "He makes a lot of money, but he'd probably play for free."

nearly every season since 1990. He always made big plays, always set himself apart as one of the best athletes on the field. But in the early days he also was prone to overzealous mistakes. Since then, his mental game has caught up to the physical, and that is why you now hear him mentioned in the same sentence as all-time greats such as Dick Butkus and Jack Lambert.

Seau has been to the last seven Pro Bowls. He has been the Chargers' leading tackler in 68 of the 141 games he has started. (He has missed only two NFL starts despite a litany of injuries, including a pinched nerve in 1994 that caused him to lose all strength in his left arm for entire quarters of play.)

"Junior Seau is the best defensive player we've faced, I'd say—and by a pretty good margin," Bill Belichick said when he coached the Cleveland Browns. "He does it all. He can play at the point of attack, he chases down plays, he plays the run, he plays the pass. He's a guy nobody's really been able to stop."

And Seau is equally unstoppable when it comes to civic activity. In 1991, he channeled his charitable efforts into the Seau Foundation, a nonprofit body that raises money for drug awareness, child abuse prevention, and college scholarships. His work won him the NFL Man of the Year award in 1994.

#55 JUNIOR SEAU, Linebacker

YEAR	TEAM	TACKLES	SACKS	FUM REC	INT	YDS	AVG	TD
1990	San Diego	85	1.0	0	0	0	—	0
1991	San Diego	129	7.0	0	0	0	—	0
1992	San Diego	102	4.5	1	2	51	25.5	0
1993	San Diego	129	0.0	1	2	58	29.0	0
1994	San Diego	155	5.5	3	0	0	—	0
1995	San Diego	129	2.0	3	2	5	2.5	0
1996	San Diego	138	7.0	3	2	18	9.0	0
1997	San Diego	97	7.0	2	2	33	16.5	0
1998	San Diego	115	3.5	2	0	0	—	0
CAREER TOTALS		1,079	37.5	15	10	165	16.5	0

Shannon Sharpe

Denver Broncos

Shannon Sharpe on gaining respect: "You're only great if you win something. I mean, Alexander wasn't Alexander the Mediocre or Alexander the Average. He was Alexander the Great, and there's a reason for it."

Shannon Sharpe on his high school education: "I didn't graduate cum laude. I graduated 'Thank you, Lawdy.' With my grades, I couldn't have gotten into prison."

Shannon Sharpe on the prospect of seeing single coverage against the Packers in Super Bowl XXXII (to a *Denver Post* columnist): "If they cover me one-on-one and beat my butt, then I will renounce my citizenship, move out of the country, and leave all my assets in a bank account in your name."

Meet the NFL's human quote machine, a seven-time Pro Bowl selection who has caught more passes for more yards than any other tight end this decade and who was instrumental to the Broncos' back-to-back victories in Super Bowls XXXII and XXXIII.

"Ever since Shannon was a little boy, there was never a dull moment," says his sister, Libby Sharpe. "Unless he was asleep."

Opponents, of course, are not always so amused. Shannon apologized to New England in 1996 after an HBO camera caught him pick-

ing up a sideline phone during a 34-8 Denver win and blurting, in mock alarm: "Mr. President, we need the National Guard, because we are killing the Patriots!"

Sharpe's act would be preposterous if he weren't able to back up his words with sensational deeds. His uncommon speed and soft hands have established him as one of the best tight ends of all time—which isn't bad for someone who spent much of his early career known as Sterling Sharpe's Little Brother.

Sterling, now a studio analyst for ESPN, was one of the most prolific wide receivers of his era. He broke the NFL single-season reception record with 108 catches in 1992, then upped the ante with 112 in 1993. But his career, once on a path to the Pro Football Hall of Fame, ended when he dislodged two vertebrae in his neck late in the 1994 season. It was a stunning blow to

> **"Ever since Shannon was a little boy, there was never a dull moment,"** says his sister, Libby Sharpe. **"Unless he was asleep."**

both Sharpes, who always have been best friends.

The two were born in Chicago, but when their neighborhood started getting too rough, their mother sent them to live with their grandparents on a farm outside of Glennville, Georgia (population: 5,000). Their nearest neighbor was a half-mile away. That meant plenty of sibling competition, and plenty of defeats for Shannon, who was three years younger.

For years, it seemed that Shannon never would emerge from his brother's shadow. Sterling received a full scholarship to South Carolina, was a first-round draft choice of the Green Bay Packers

in 1988, and burst onto the scene with a total of 145 catches in his first three NFL seasons. Shannon wound up at Division II Savannah State. He went in the seventh round (the 192nd overall pick) in the NFL draft as a wide receiver to the Broncos in 1990, and caught a total of 29 passes in his first two years. He was one game away from being cut as a rookie, but responded with an inspired performance in the Broncos' final preseason game.

Then-head coach Dan Reeves is credited with encouraging Shannon and converting him to tight end. Once at the bigger position, he began a gradual ascension to stardom.

What held Sharpe back in the first place? It may have been that sports was just too easy for him. He averaged 30 points and 15 rebounds as a high school basketball player, and won the Georgia state championship with a triple jump of 49 feet 5 inches. It wasn't until he decided to devote himself completely to football that he blossomed.

Sharpe started haunting the Broncos' weight room, and it wasn't long before he was sporting 21-inch biceps, a 52-inch chest, and a body-fat count of 4 percent. "It's tough to match up with Shannon," former Broncos quarterback John Elway says. "There aren't many guys who can bump Shannon because he's too strong for them."

And there are fewer, especially among linebackers and strong safeties, who can run with him stride for stride. Sharpe led all NFL tight ends with 72 catches for 1,107 yards in 1997, and had 10 touchdown catches in both 1996 and '98.

"He's one of the five best players in the league," New York Jets head coach Bill Parcells says.

#84 SHANNON SHARPE, Tight End

YEAR	TEAM	NO	YDS	AVG	TD
1990	Denver	7	99	14.1	1
1991	Denver	22	322	14.6	1
1992	Denver	53	640	12.1	2
1993	Denver	81	995	12.3	9
1994	Denver	87	1,010	11.6	4
1995	Denver	63	756	12.0	4
1996	Denver	80	1,062	13.3	10
1997	Denver	72	1,107	15.4	3
1998	Denver	64	768	12.0	10
CAREER TOTALS		529	6,759	12.8	44

Bruce Smith

Buffalo Bills

When quarterback Jeff George has nightmares, there's a good chance they'll involve a game he played while with the Colts in 1990. It seemed as though every time George dropped back to pass that day, Buffalo's Bruce Smith was in his face. By the end of the game, Smith had dropped George 4 times.

If George can take any solace in such a pounding, it's in the fact that he has plenty of company. Fifty-eight NFL quarterbacks, from Steve Grogan to Jeff Blake, have found themselves buried beneath Smith since 1985. Surely, more victims await number 78.

Smith is the perfect pass-rushing machine. At 6 feet 4 inches, 273 pounds, with hardly an ounce of fat, he moves like a hungry velociraptor.

"He has an unbelievably explosive first step," says Patriots tackle Bruce Armstrong, a long-time rival and admirer. "He's relentless, and once you get into him you must stay on him because he has such great closing speed. He can get to the quarterback even when you think the ball should be gone."

A native of Norfolk, Virginia, Smith put the Virginia Tech football program on the map. He won the Outland Trophy as the nation's best collegiate lineman in 1984 and the Bills made him the first pick in the

1985 draft. He started immediately, and by 1987 he was earning the first of 10 Pro Bowl bids. (Among NFL defensive ends, only Reggie White has more.)

Smith has been consistently excellent throughout

his career, but his 1990 season stands out. It was then he terrorized NFL passers for a career-high 19 sacks and 4 forced fumbles. He helped Buffalo make it to Super Bowl XXV, where he staked the team to a 12-3 lead by tackling Giants quarterback Jeff Hostetler for a safety. (The Bills eventually lost 20-19.)

During the 1990 season, Smith declared himself Lawrence Taylor's successor as the best defensive player in the league.

> "I demand attention. I feel that the only way I'll get better is if I have at least two people on me. It makes me rise to the occasion."

That did not sit well in some circles, but those close to Smith know he wasn't boasting. He simply was pointing out what the average fan might not see: the double- and triple-team blocks he constantly faces.

"I consider it an insult if it doesn't happen," Smith says about the tag-teaming. "I demand attention. I feel that the only way I'll get better is if I have at least two people on me. It makes me rise to the occasion."

Anyway, Smith's claim was hard to contradict. Some said he was purely a speed rusher; they never had to play against him. "Most people think that because he's so quick he has only an outside pass rush," says veteran quarterback Warren Moon (sacked 6 times, tied for sixth on the Smith List). "But he's so powerful he can bulldoze over you."

A more common complaint claimed Smith was weak against the ground game. That may have been true early in his career, but his run defense has improved greatly over the years. He has recorded four seasons with 100-plus tackles, the most ever among Bills defensive linemen.

And as the millennium approaches, Smith is busy proving one more thing: endurance. "He knows he's good, and it's fun to do something you're good at," says Marv Levy, who retired as Bills head coach after the 1997 season. "He must have a great thirst for the game to be playing with this much vigor for this long."

In 1998, his fourteenth NFL season, Smith missed the season opener at San Diego with a knee injury but still went on to record 10 sacks and once again was on his way to Honolulu. Only White (192½) has more career sacks than Smith's 164, and they share the all-time postseason record of 12. (Sacks have been an official NFL statistic since 1982.) Smith and White are the only defenders to record at least 10 sacks in 12 different seasons. Yet Smith still is able to leave the young guys shaking their heads.

As rookie defensive end Marcellus Wiley reported in 1997, "People were telling me, 'Wait until you see Bruce do some things. You think we're good players? Wait until you see Bruce.' He amazed me from the first snap."

#78 BRUCE SMITH, Defensive End

YEAR	TEAM	TACKLES	SACKS	FUM REC	INT	YDS	AVG	TD
1985	Buffalo	48	6.5	4	0	0	—	0
1986	Buffalo	63	15.0	0	0	0	—	0
1987	Buffalo	78	12.0	2	0	0	—	0
1988	Buffalo	56	11.0	0	0	0	—	0
1989	Buffalo	88	13.0	0	0	0	—	0
1990	Buffalo	101	19.0	0	0	0	—	0
1991	Buffalo	18	1.5	0	0	0	—	0
1992	Buffalo	89	14.0	0	0	0	—	0
1993	Buffalo	108	14.0	1	1	0	0.0	0
1994	Buffalo	92	10.0	2	1	0	0.0	0
1995	Buffalo	107	10.5	1	0	0	—	0
1996	Buffalo	120	13.5	1	0	0	—	0
1997	Buffalo	87	14.0	0	0	0	—	0
1998	Buffalo	74	10.0	2	0	0	—	0
CAREER TOTALS		1,129	164.0	13	2	0	0.0	0

Emmitt Smith

Dallas Cowboys

Only three times has a running back won both an NFL rushing title and a Super Bowl championship in the same season. The three players who did it were Emmitt Smith, Emmitt Smith, and Emmitt Smith.

Before Smith rolled deuces in 1992, 1993, and 1995, some considered it an unattainable feat. Relying so heavily on a single person, they claimed, makes a team too one-dimensional. But Smith's versatility and durability, not to mention a roster of talented teammates, made him unique.

"When you have to go with a running back who is the complete back—receiving, blocking, and running—I feel Emmitt is the guy," says Franco Harris, a Hall of Fame runner for the Pittsburgh Steelers in their championship seasons.

Smith's impact on the Cowboys has been immense. When he held out to start the 1993 season, the team dropped its first two games, to Washington and Buffalo. Smith saw Dallas head coach Jimmy Johnson looking weary and anxious on television, and he decided it was time to return. No team ever had overcome an 0-2 start to win the Super Bowl, but with Smith leading the way—he would win his third rushing title—the Cowboys went 12-2 over the remainder of the regular season and waltzed through the postseason.

Playing Buffalo in Super Bowl XXVIII at the end of the year, the Cowboys found themselves trailing 13-6 at halftime. So they put the ball in Smith's hands and watched him sink the Bills with 91 second-half yards. He finished with 132 yards and 2 touchdowns, and was named most valuable player of the game.

"Emmitt was making so many pretty moves, he

was about to shake me out of my drawers," Dallas guard Nate Newton said afterward.

Smith has a full assortment of shakes and bakes, but he isn't a magician along the lines of Barry Sanders. And that's Emmitt in a nutshell: not the very best at any one category, but good at everything. He isn't a bulldozer at 214 pounds, but he is shockingly powerful for his size. Ask former 49ers linebacker Bill Romanowski, whom Smith flattened to set up the go-ahead touchdown in the 1992 NFC Championship Game.

Smith's speed could be described as adequate. As

Whitey Jordan, his offensive coordinator at Florida, said, "He may not go eighty yards on one play, but he can go forty yards twice."

Really, Smith's skills are harder to pinpoint. "What separates him from other backs is explosiveness," Dallas quarterback Troy Aikman says. "Once he gets the ball, he has tremendous vision. He's hard to bring down because he's so strong in his hips and his legs."

Smith's most important body part, though, is his oversized heart. That vital organ was never more in evidence than on January 2, 1994. Visiting the Giants in the last week of the season, with the NFC

> "Emmitt was making so many pretty moves, he was about to shake me out of my drawers."
> — Nate Newton

East title and home-field playoff advantage on the line, Smith suffered a first-degree separation of his right shoulder in the first half. The pain was excruciating. His teammates had to help him up after every carry. But Smith would not relent. He handled the ball 17 times after the injury and led Dallas to a 16-13 overtime victory, gaining 41 of the Cowboys' 52 yards on the winning drive.

It's difficult to believe, but by 1997 some people questioned whether Smith still had what it takes to be a premier NFL running back.

True, he had his seventh consecutive 1,000-yard

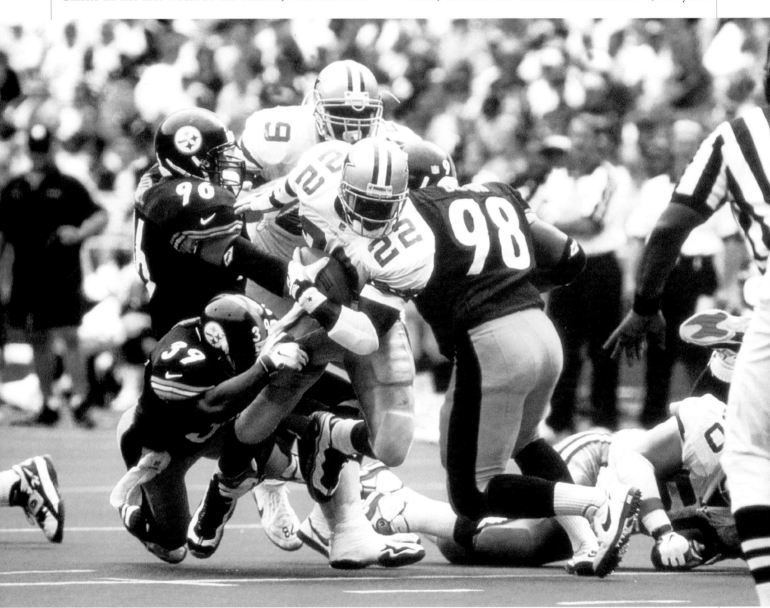

rushing season, but his 1,074 yards that year represented his lowest total since his rookie season in 1990. And his 4 rushing touchdowns were by far the fewest in his career.

"For all athletes, everybody's always quick to say, 'He's lost it. He's not this. He's not that,'" Aikman says. "Certainly, a lot of people were saying that about Emmitt. But he's still a great football player."

Smith proved that with a vengeance in 1998, bouncing back to rush for 1,332 yards and 13 touchdowns while making the Pro Bowl for the first time since 1995 (the sixth time in his career). By season's end, he ranked fifth on the NFL's all-time rushing list with 12,566 yards.

"When somebody says something bad about you, you want to prove them wrong," he says. "I've got plenty of gas left in my tank, and plenty of tread on my tires."

But it is hard to remember this gritty, win-at-all-costs competitor when Smith is standing in a school auditorium. Kids love the guy. His modest height (5 feet 9 inches) and elfin grin make him look more like a mascot than a football player. But as Smith hit the circuit of schools in the Dallas–Fort Worth area, something began to bug him. Here he was telling students to stay in school, and he didn't have a college diploma—he had left Florida 13 units shy of his degree. So Smith fulfilled a promise to his mother and went back to school, earning a bachelor's degree in public recreation in May, 1996.

Smith has had a lifetime full of honors. He gained 8,804 yards (third best ever among preps) at Escambia High School in Pensacola, Florida; he set 58 school records in three years at the University of Florida; he is one of only four NFL players to win three consecutive rushing titles; he set an NFL record with 25 touchdowns in 1995; he owns the league postseason mark for career touchdowns (20); he was portrayed, along with the legendary Red Grange, on the cover of a book that celebrated the league's seventy-fifth anniversary; he has three Super Bowl rings.

But the diploma was special. Above all, it was a measure of resilience, which is what Emmitt Smith is all about.

#22 EMMITT SMITH, Running Back

| YEAR | TEAM | RUSHING | | | | RECEIVING | | | |
		NO	YDS	AVG	TD	NO	YDS	AVG	TD
1990	Dallas	241	937	3.9	11	24	228	9.5	0
1991	Dallas	365	1,563	4.3	12	49	258	5.3	1
1992	Dallas	373	1,713	4.6	18	59	335	5.7	1
1993	Dallas	283	1,486	5.3	9	57	414	7.3	1
1994	Dallas	368	1,484	4.0	21	50	341	6.8	1
1995	Dallas	377	1,773	4.7	25	62	375	6.1	0
1996	Dallas	327	1,204	3.7	12	47	249	5.3	3
1997	Dallas	261	1,074	4.1	4	40	234	5.9	0
1998	Dallas	319	1,332	4.2	13	27	175	6.5	2
CAREER TOTALS		2,914	12,566	4.3	125	415	2,609	6.3	9

Michael Strahan

New York Giants

Reggie White and Bruce Smith may be the greatest defensive ends ever to play in the NFL at the same time. For years they hounded quarterbacks from opposite conferences, delighting fans and racking up sacks. The only problem was, it started to look as though a successor would never emerge.

Finally, with White retired and Smith chugging along at 36, the new wave has arrived. His name is Michael Strahan, and practically nobody saw him coming.

Strahan was a longshot of improbable odds, primarily because he grew up in Germany, the son of a U.S. Army man. Michael and his father, Gene, would get up at 4 A.M. on Tuesday mornings to watch tape-delayed broadcasts of *Monday Night Football*. But Michael stopped playing the sport in the eighth grade, when he ran out of suitable competition.

"People in Germany just didn't play football," Strahan says. "And Germans definitely don't think of going to college to play football."

Still, Michael was big and athletic, which gave Gene an idea. He sent his son to Texas for the first semester of his senior year of high school. Michael played football for Westbury High and lived with his uncle, Art Strahan, a defensive lineman for parts of two seasons with the Oilers and Falcons in the 1960s. It was just a

taste, but enough to get Michael hungering for football stardom.

The major colleges didn't exactly come knocking for the inexperienced young athlete. Strahan wound

up at Texas Southern, a predominately black Division 1-AA school. He was raw, but he learned enough to set a TSU record with 19 sacks as a senior. That, combined with crisp workouts and a strong showing at the Senior Bowl, convinced the New York Giants to draft him in the second round in 1993.

"I remember the first time my rookie year when they introduced LT [legendary linebacker Lawrence Taylor] coming out of the tunnel," Strahan says. "I had hair rise up in places I didn't even know I had hair."

Some young players, such as Minnesota wide receiver Randy Moss, hit the NFL with the impact of a meteorite. Michael Strahan arrived like a glacier—slowly, methodically…but unstoppably.

Strahan saw little action as a rookie. He started 15 games in 1994, but still toiled in relative anonymity. He got a little better in 1995, posting 7 1/2 sacks. And then John Fox was hired as defensive coordinator in 1997. Fox implemented an analytical, aggressive defense, and Strahan blossomed,

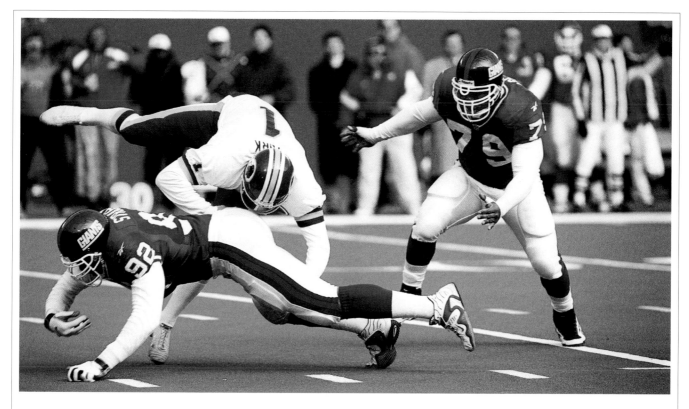

picking up 29 sacks over the next two seasons.

Suddenly, football fans everywhere woke up to the 6-foot 5-inch, 272-pound defensive end with the impish smile. Those who listened closely were treated to an intelligent and friendly athlete who takes in stray dogs and rarely refuses an autograph.

On the field, Strahan is a multidimensional player, one of the few defensive ends who can use either brute strength or agile moves to get to the passer, then stuff the run with equal verve. Fox sometimes drops him back into pass coverage, as he did against Washington in 1998, when Strahan intercepted a pass and returned it 24 yards for a touchdown. The Giants acknowledged his importance in August, 1999, signing him to a four-year contract extension that made him the NFL's highest paid defensive lineman.

So is he the best?

"I can't say that," Strahan says. "That would sound boastful."

Others are happy to say it for him. "He's definitely the best defensive lineman in the NFL," Giants safety Sam Garnes says. "Before you get to the NFL you hear a lot of stuff about a lot of guys, and not all of them are as good as you hear. But getting to see him every week, it's all true. He brings his best every single week."

Now Strahan receives the ultimate interior-line compliment: constant double-teaming by opposing blockers. "I've seen tackle-guard, tackle-tight end, tackle-back, tight end-back and, worst of all, tackle-tight end-back," he says. "It's a part of the game for me. A bad part."

Of course, there are a lot of good parts to the game, and Strahan openly enjoys his profession. He and his father, who remained in Germany with the family to run a transport business, still laugh about the crazy route Michael took to get here.

"The true lesson is that it's not how you start, it's how you finish," the defensive end says, "and I'm finishing pretty well."

#92 MICHAEL STRAHAN, Defensive End

YEAR	TEAM	TACKLES	SACKS	FUM REC	INT	YDS	AVG	TD
1993	N.Y. Giants	3	1.0	0	0	0	—	0
1994	N.Y. Giants	39	4.5	0	0	0	—	0
1995	N.Y. Giants	58	7.5	0	2	56	28.0	0
1996	N.Y. Giants	63	5.0	0	0	0	—	0
1997	N.Y. Giants	69	14.0	1	0	0	—	0
1998	N.Y. Giants	67	15.0	0	1	24	24.0	1
CAREER TOTALS		299	47.0	1	3	80	26.7	1

Derrick Thomas

Kansas City Chiefs

Derrick Thomas is a Chief, but he also is a falcon. Make that *the* falcon.

Kansas City defensive coordinator Gunther Cunningham (now the head coach), unhappy with his unit's performance in 1996, rewrote some 500 pages of the Chiefs' playbook for 1997. The new base defense was called the Falcon, and it revolved around a position of the same name. The man who fills that position is Thomas, who resembles nothing more than a swift bird of prey when zeroing in on NFL quarterbacks.

"You have to know where he is at every moment on the football field," Broncos head coach Mike Shanahan says. "There are few players you can say that about."

The whole point of the Falcon is to make Thomas hard to locate. He may line up as the right defensive end in a three-point stance. He may be a stand-up linebacker on the left side. He may even drop into pass coverage.

Unfortunately, Thomas did not get to take full advantage of his new opportunities. He missed six starts while recovering from a torn triceps in 1997. Still, that didn't stop him from recording 9½ sacks (tied for sixth in the AFC) and making the Pro Bowl for the ninth time in his nine-year career. He had 12 sacks in 1998, when he also forced 3 fumbles and recovered 2

(he returned 1 of them 44 yards for a touchdown).

Thomas was the first player selected under head coach Marty Schottenheimer and general manager Carl Peterson, a regime that has taken the Chiefs to seven playoff appearances since 1989. And in that span he has collected sacks the way some people collect Beanie Babies. Thomas currently ranks ninth on the all-time list with 119½. He set the single-game record by sacking Seattle's Dave Krieg 7 times in 1990, a performance that helped him total 20 for the season. The speed of his assaults has resulted in 42 forced fumbles during his career. He also has recovered 18 fumbles.

Half of Thomas's work is accomplished with a lightning-fast first

"As great an athlete as he is, it is the stuff he does away from the game that stands out to me. That is what makes him a really big man."
— Chris Martin

step. "You have your fast outside linebackers who pass rush in a Nickel situation," retired tackle Anthony Muñoz said, "and then you've got Derrick Thomas, who is pretty much in a class by himself. I've never really played against a guy who had that initial quickness off the ball."

About the only place Thomas can be found as frequently as the

opponent's backfield is in the various branches of the Kansas City public library.

His signature social program is Third and Long, a literacy campaign that he promotes by spending each home Saturday of the football season in a library, reading to underprivileged kids. His work won him the 1993 NFL Man of the Year Award and the 1995 Byron White Humanitarian Award, the latter from the NFL Players Association.

"As great an athlete as he is, it is the stuff he does away from the game that stands out to me," former Chiefs linebacker Chris Martin says. "That is what makes him a really big man."

Thomas received another honor when he was asked to present the keynote address at the Memorial Day observance in 1993 at the Vietnam War Memorial. His father, Robert Thomas, was an Air Force captain whose B-52 bomber was shot down over Vietnam in December, 1972, when Derrick was 5 years old. The mission for which Robert Thomas gave his life, strangely enough, was called Operation Linebacker Two.

Other than a father, Derrick had everything a child needs to get by, but that didn't prevent him from making a lot of bad decisions in his junior high and early high school years. He lived near the projects in Miami, close enough to find trouble without looking for it.

"I had one-thousand-dollar bikes sitting at my house," Thomas says, "but I wanted to go out with my friends and steal a bike that was probably worth less than fifty dollars."

That came to an end when a judge sentenced him to a stint in the Dade Marine Institute, a state-run alternative school for troubled teens. There were no frills at DMI, and his time there showed him a path he did not want to travel.

"When I got back to high school, I had to make a decision on what I was going to do," Thomas says. "Was I going to be a positive member or a negative member of society? Positive growth won out."

Years later, Thomas's positive growth continues to result in negative yardage for the quarterbacks of the NFL.

#58 DERRICK THOMAS, Linebacker

YEAR	TEAM	TACKLES	SACKS	FUM REC	INT	YDS	AVG	TD
1989	Kansas City	75	10.0	1	0	0	—	0
1990	Kansas City	63	20.0	2	0	0	—	0
1991	Kansas City	79	13.5	4	0	0	—	0
1992	Kansas City	67	14.5	3	0	0	—	0
1993	Kansas City	43	8.0	1	0	0	—	0
1994	Kansas City	86	11.0	3	0	0	—	0
1995	Kansas City	71	8.0	1	0	0	—	0
1996	Kansas City	58	13.0	1	0	0	—	0
1997	Kansas City	55	9.5	0	0	0	—	0
1998	Kansas City	54	12.0	2	0	0	—	0
CAREER TOTALS		651	119.5	18	0	0	—	0

Aeneas Williams

Arizona Cardinals

At a family Christmas gathering a few years ago, Aeneas Williams's aunt played an audiotape she had found lying around. Aeneas had made the recording on his Mr. Microphone toy as a child, but had forgotten about it. On the tape was a boy's innocent voice declaring, "I'm going to be a pro football player someday, and I'm going to be the best defensive back in the NFL."

It was quite a boast. Then again, it was quite a young man who made it. Thanks to a stable family—especially his disciplinarian father, a lab supervisor for Union Carbide—Williams emerged from one of New Orleans's toughest school systems to earn his place as a Pro Bowl cornerback and a solid citizen.

"My father always told us, 'If you have to choose between me and the police, you'd better choose the police,'" Williams says.

In the long run, Williams chose God, football, and community service. One of four teammates at Fortier High School who eventually would play defensive back in the NFL—the others were Ashley Ambrose, Maurice Hurst, and Kevin Lewis—he was offered an academic scholarship to Dartmouth. But Williams turned down the Ivy League, opting to follow his brother Achilles to Southern University. (Aeneas and Achilles, you may know, were characters glorified by the Greek poet Homer in *The Iliad*. As Aeneas Williams says, "We had the Trojan War in our backyard every weekend.")

Aeneas did not attend Southern to play sports. He took accounting classes and got involved in student government for two years before he decided to try football. By his senior year (when he played as a graduate student, having already earned his degree) he tied for the NCAA Division

I-AA lead with 11 interceptions.

Williams started for the Cardinals as a 1991 rookie and never looked back. He has played in the last five Pro Bowls. He led the NFC in interceptions in 1994 and tied for the lead in 1991. And he helped lead the Cardinals to their first playoff appearance in 16 years (and their first postseason victory in 51 years) in 1998.

"He might be the best I've been around," says Buddy Ryan, his head coach in 1994–95. "He can do it all. He can tackle. He can cover. He can run. He takes a challenge."

No one challenged him more than Ryan, whose attacking 46 defense forced its cornerbacks into steady man-for-man coverage. And remember, at 5 feet 10 inches Williams gives up size to the likes of Dallas's Michael Irvin (6-2) and Washington's Michael Westbrook (6-3). Williams hasn't backed down yet.

"With Aeneas you know it's going to be good, clean, hard-nosed football," says another friendly rival, the Redskins' Irving Fryar. "It's always a joy to be able to go out and compete against a guy like that."

Opposing quarterbacks might not find the experience as joyful. More and more of them are being victimized by what Williams calls the "quick six." Six times he has returned interceptions for touchdowns—only 3 away from Ken Houston's all-time record.

Williams actually called Houston a few years ago to pick his brain about techniques and strategy. But that is nothing new. Williams, an avid student of the game, has sought out veterans such as Gill Byrd, Ronnie Lott, and Everson Walls to compare notes.

Williams works hard on his conditioning, too. He keeps himself in such good shape that he was the only Cardinals player to post a sub-2-minute time when the team opened its 1994 training camp with a mandatory 880-yard run. "I hate mediocrity," he says. "I disdain 'average' with a passion. If I feel there's an area where I'm average, then I'm

> **"I hate mediocrity. I disdain 'average' with a passion. If I feel there's an area where I'm average, then I'm going to go to the woodshed and find out how I can raise my level."**

going to go to the woodshed and find out how I can raise my level."

When it comes to his personal life, Williams shouldn't spend any time in that woodshed. He gets up at 5 A.M. every day to pray and read the Bible, and he hosts a weekly Bible study for teammates and their wives. He also doesn't drink, and he doesn't swear.

"I've told young players who come in here," Arizona defensive backs coach Larry Marmie says, "'If you're going to pick somebody to follow, watch this guy. Watch him in the meetings, watch him on the practice field, and watch him in the game.'"

Above all, watch him on the quick-out pattern, or he's liable to burn you for a quick six.

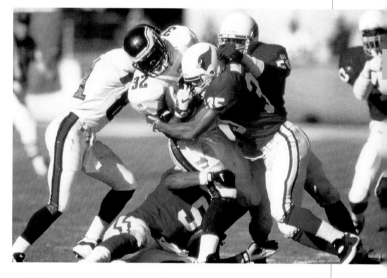

#35 AENEAS WILLIAMS, Cornerback

YEAR	TEAM	TACKLES	SACKS	FUM REC	INT	YDS	AVG	TD
1991	Phoenix	48	0.0	1	6	60	10.0	0
1992	Phoenix	48	0.0	1	3	25	8.3	0
1993	Phoenix	42	0.0	2	2	87	43.5	1
1994	Arizona	46	0.0	1	9	89	9.9	0
1995	Arizona	58	0.0	3	6	86	14.3	2
1996	Arizona	74	1.0	1	6	89	14.8	1
1997	Arizona	70	0.0	0	6	95	15.8	2
1998	Arizona	85	1.0	0	1	15	15.0	0
CAREER TOTALS		**471**	**2.0**	**9**	**39**	**546**	**14.0**	**6**

Steve Young

Steve Young was riding high when he left Brigham Young University in 1984. Not only had he set an NCAA record by completing 71.3 percent of his passes as a senior, he was a great-great-great-grandson of Brigham Young, Mormon patriarch and the man for whom the school is named. Talk about a campus hero!

But Young shunned the NFL and signed instead with the Los Angeles Express of the United States Football League. It wasn't what you'd call a great career move. The USFL foundered financially and couldn't consistently attract large crowds. For a developing young quarterback, it must have seemed that things couldn't get worse.

They did.

The Tampa Bay Buccaneers made Young the first pick in the 1984 supplemental draft, and the left-handed passer soon found himself running for his life behind a rickety offensive line. He went 4-15 as a starter during two seasons with Tampa Bay, throwing 11 touchdown passes against 21 interceptions. Again, things couldn't get any worse.

Again, they did.

Most players would have relished a trade to the powerful 49ers in 1987, but for a quarterback it meant sitting on the bench while Joe Montana performed his miracles. In his first four seasons in San Francisco, Young started only 10 games. He grew increasingly impatient. By the end of the 1990 season, he was 29 years old and wondering when he'd be an NFL starter.

It happened the next season as Montana recuperated from elbow surgery. It would prove to be a painful time for both men.

No matter what Young did in his first three seasons by the Bay—and he led the NFL in passer rating all three years—the fans (not to mention some of his teammates) would not accept him. They moaned about Young not getting the ball to Jerry Rice enough, about his frequent downfield runs, and his inability to win the big games.

A less stable individual would have caved in under the pressure. But Young is a fun-loving prankster who used to tell his Express center, Mike

Ruether, "Snap the ball over my head, and let's see what happens."

Young continued to speak with his actions, and he turned the corner in 1994, when he bolstered his individual excellence with a victory in Super Bowl XXIX. He even set a Super Bowl record with 6 touchdown passes in the 49ers' 49-26 win over San Diego. Finally, this was his team.

The funny part is, Young has no regrets about his early hurdles. "The Buccaneers were worthwhile," he says. "The Express was worthwhile. Now I feel like all those trials and struggles kind of make sitting on top of the mountain a nicer place to be."

The view from that mountaintop must be something else. In a purely statistical index, Young is the greatest quarterback in NFL history. It isn't even close. After leading the league with a rating of 104.7 in 1997, he joined Sammy Baugh as the only men ever to win 6 NFL passing titles. In the 79-year history of the league, only 26 times has a quarterback exceeded a rating of 100 in a season; 6 of them belong to Young. Montana, with three 100+ seasons, is the only other passer with more than one. And of the two, Young actually has the better winning percentage in San Francisco, .736 to .719.

Brigham Young's descendant has emerged as an unflappable leader and an accurate passer.

"He can throw the three levels of ball—the three-step, eight-to-fifteen yards, and the line of scrimmage to infinity—with ability," says Milt Davis, an NFL scout for 30 years. "Not too many can do all three well."

Not many have Young's mobility, either. Some have called him a running back with an arm. Among quarterbacks, only Randall Cunningham has run for more yardage than Young's 4,182, and no one has scored more touchdowns than Young's 43 (he surpassed Jack Kemp's 40 in 1998).

Yet he is the same down-to-earth guy whom teammate Harris Barton once jokingly accused of tossing each new trophy and game ball he

> "The Buccaneers were worthwhile. The Express was worthwhile. Now I feel like all those trials and struggles kind of make sitting on top of the mountain a nicer place to be."

earned into the back seat of his car. Young takes constant ribbing because of his taste for inexpensive clothes and used automobiles. Don't be fooled, though. He also is a sharp-witted student who earned his law degree from BYU in 1994. He claimed he took the classes to keep from getting bored in the offseason.

"The thing that keeps me young is the constant quest for perfection," he says.

#8 STEVE YOUNG, Quarterback

YEAR	TEAM	ATT	COMP	PCT	YDS	TD	INT	RATING
1985	Tampa Bay	138	72	52.2	935	3	8	56.9
1986	Tampa Bay	363	195	53.7	2,282	8	13	65.5
1987	San Francisco	69	37	53.6	570	10	0	120.8
1988	San Francisco	101	54	53.5	680	3	3	72.2
1989	San Francisco	92	64	69.6	1,001	8	3	120.8
1990	San Francisco	62	38	61.3	427	2	0	92.6
1991	San Francisco	279	180	64.5	2,517	17	8	101.8
1992	San Francisco	402	268	66.7	3,465	25	7	107.0
1993	San Francisco	462	314	68.0	4,023	29	16	101.5
1994	San Francisco	461	324	70.3	3,969	35	10	112.8
1995	San Francisco	447	299	66.9	3,200	20	11	92.3
1996	San Francisco	316	214	67.7	2,410	14	6	97.2
1997	San Francisco	356	241	67.7	3,029	19	6	104.7
1998	San Francisco	517	322	62.3	4,170	36	12	101.1
CAREER TOTALS		4,065	2,622	64.5	32,678	229	103	97.6

PHOTO CREDITS

Bill Amatucci 23, 54, 57, 91, 140

James V. Biever 26, 62, 66

Peter Brouillet 13, 28, 48, 126, 141

Chris Covatta 65, 83, 121

Jimmy Cribb 97

Greg Crisp 67, 79, 120, 123

Tom Croke 88

Scott Cunningham 15

David Drapkin 59, 96, 115, 117, 128

Mike Eliason 43, 100, 106

Gerald Gallegos 70, 112, 113

E.B. Graphics 147

George Gojkovich 77, 116

Seth Harrison 35

Thearon Henderson 85

Glenn James 6, 69

Paul Jasienski 31, 37, 110, 111, 150

Allen Kee 41, 73, 80, 87, 92, 104, 107, 118, 132, 153

Al Kooistra 136

L.C. Lambrecht 22, 90

Richard Mackson 10

Michael Martin 51, 146

Al Messerschmidt 71, 95, 151

Darrell McAllister 42, 68

Tom Miller 20, 56, 144

Mike Moore 105

Marty Morrow 29

Steven Murphy 27, 39, 44, 86, 142

Bernie Nuñez 93, 135

Al Pereira 133

Richard Pilling 138

Evan Pinkus 9

Joe Poellot 45, 52, 53, 129

Louis Raynor 149

Mitchell B. Reibel 17, 19, 49, 74, 134, 139, 143

Joe Robbins 46, 82

Bob Rosato 30, 33, 38, 78, 84, 114, 122, 152

Todd Rosenberg 7, 64

John Sandhaus 16, 47

James D. Smith 8, 11, 36, 101

Paul Spinelli/NFLP 24, 76, 109, 127, 156

Allen Dean Steele 12

David Stock 14

David Stluka 25, 50, 58, 60, 61, 98, 102, 125, 148, 157

Kevin Terrell/NFLP 63

Greg Trott 32, 34, 81, 119, 124, 130, 131

Tony Tomsic 103

Jim Turner 40, 72, 75, 89, 137

Ron Vesely 21, 55, 94, 99

R.C. Waclawicz 145

Paul Williams 18

Michael Zagaris 1, 108, 154, 155